PRAISE FOR *START WITH HEART*

"In *Start with Heart*, Bill Crouch boils down decades of experience into an easy-to-read yet meaty collection of helpful tips, guidelines, and tools that is sure to help anyone become a better fundraiser and any organization shore up its endowment."

GREG WARNER
CEO and founder of MarketSmart

"Working with Bill through the years, I know that his core message is that fundraising is all about the heart. At Bethesda, we have learned so much from him and the BrightDot approach. *Start with Heart* is highly recommended for any development program wishing to raise more money and more friends."

LORENE KING
Vice president of philanthropy
of Bethesda Lutheran Communities

"As chairman of the board of the Georgetown College Foundation for 12 years, I worked with Bill Crouch where together we raised millions of dollars, built new facilities, created a faculty development fund, grew the endowment, and more. We employed the principles Bill now shares with you in *Start with Heart*. This book's proven and successful methods were effective with a diverse group of donors, and they are on target for small college development offices and fundraising endeavors generally."

CARL ARTHUR HENLEIN, ESQ

D1714493

"*Start with Heart* is deeply inspiring, and I believe every leader of people needs to read it and start to immediately implement the principles. There is no doubt in my mind if these principles were applied to all teams there would be a transformation of people, organizations, and our world."

JENNIFER GIORDANO
Leadership consultant and CEO of SmartfulWorks

"When we follow our hearts, we can forge authentic relationships that spur all sorts of accomplishments—even in fundraising. This book provides proven methods and inspiring examples of real-life development professionals who have learned these valuable lessons and scored enormous victories. The process, the work, and the rewards feel different—more positive and more rewarding—when we start with heart."

DR. JO ALLEN
President of Meredith College

"BrightDot's methods have helped transform our board's culture, and I use them every day to engage my staff as well as our donors and other partners. They work!"

BARBARA MULKEY
Director of Shelton Leadership Center,
North Carolina State University

"This important book offers a fresh and needed change in fundraising perspective—from the merely transactional to the truly transformational. As important as technical proficiency is to the craft, what matters most are the underlying relationships, thoughtfully and humanely developed."

CARROLL D. STEVENS
Emeritus vice president of advancement at Claremont McKenna College and former associate dean for development at Yale Law School

Start
WITH
Heart

Start WITH Heart

The Secret Power of Emotions to Catalyze Fundraising Results
for Individuals, Teams, and Organizations

BILL CROUCH
FOUNDER AND CEO OF BRIGHTDOT

BrightDot
PRESS

Start with Heart

The Secret Power of Emotions
to Catalyze Fundraising Results
for Individuals, Teams, and Organizations
By Bill Crouch

Visit us at www.thebrightdot.com

For speaking requests or to inquire about single or quantity orders of START WITH HEART, please email us at info@thebrightdot.com

Published by BrightDot Press, Raleigh, NC, USA.
Printed in the United States of America
First edition

Book collaboration by Wanda Urbanska.
Concept and editorial development by Janet Goldstein.
Cover and book design | Yvonne Parks | PearCreative.ca

ISBN (Print): 978-1-7341044-0-0

ISBN (eBook): 978-1-7341044-1-7

DEDICATION

This book is dedicated to those individuals who joined with me over the past five years with a dream to impact millions of lives across the United States by empowering nonprofits and higher education institutions to raise more money so they can serve more people.

And to Jan, my wife, who stands beside me, encourages me every day, and models to our grandchildren the importance of servant leadership.

CONTENTS

Acknowledgments 13

The Foundations:
A New Framework 17

The Realities:
The Hard Work of Heart 27

Principle #1
Find the Joy 37

Principle #2
Create Messages That Connect 61

Principle #3
Tap the Power of Emotional Intelligence 97

Afterword 129

About Bill Crouch and BrightDot 133

ACKNOWLEDGMENTS

This book began after a conversation in Chicago with Jerry Panas, who encouraged me to start my own firm, which eventually became a reality and led me to hone the theories, methodologies, and practices I had spent a lifetime pressure-testing in my fundraising, leadership, and, later, consulting roles with the BrightDot team. The wisdom and encouragement I received from him were priceless.

A plane conversation with Dr. Katharine Leslie began to put feet to the dream, followed by a discussion with Dr. Carol Pate that led to the significant research that underlies all we do. A meeting with Cleve Folger on the back deck of the Country Club at Wakefield Plantation gave me the courage to step out with my own firm and brought me to Hardy Dail, who joined me in the BrightDot mission and who has been my stabilizer.

A meeting with Michael Strader showed me how to implement our work, and a follow-up visit with Scott

Koskoski brought us another team member to help spread the word of our unique work. Sherri Stewart brought her insights of emotional intelligence to my attention. Theo Pikes opened my eyes to the complex challenges of diversity. Nancy Rieves offered us stellar fundraising expertise. Meg Foley challenged us with conversations about breaking through the status quo. Lauren Pesce brought us knowledge about special events. Wanda Urbanska joined the team as our content specialist. Shelley Burdine-Prevost brought smiles to all our faces along with psychology expertise. Kim Turner opened up a new region for us. Jessi Marsh became another implementor and Carolyn Walters and Katey Zeh risked with us on a new venture. Dontrese Brown has kept us all looking good and sharp with his corporate marketing genius. Erin Jackson has focused on client relations, and Mamie Sutphin continues to be a strategic advisor. And I would be remiss not to acknowledge the contributions of my five children who have offered both encouragement and keen insights that have helped guide the way.

Without each one of these individual's investment along the way, BrightDot would not be the dynamic firm it is today—with a singular focus on a new approach to fundraising success for individuals and organizations.

I also want to call out our masterminds—those friends, critics, and encouragers who have given of their time and business acumen to keep us on track. A big thank you to Larry Smith, Scott Neal, and Carl Henlein!

Building on the foundational work of the BrightDot firm, this book brings to fruition a key tenet of everything we do: start with heart. Wanda Urbanska, whose heart and book-writing skills are amazing, took this project under her wing and worked alongside—and sometimes even ahead of—me through the entire process. I can't thank her enough.

I am grateful to Janet Goldstein who brought her publishing acumen and creative skills to our team as we envisioned this book. She pushed and prodded me to reach deep to find the lessons and stories that would inspire others.

In addition, I want to thank Dontrese Brown, Adrienne Faraci, and Yvonne Park who helped manage the details and make everything look just right.

Finally, I'm indebted to all our clients and colleagues, especially those who shared the stories in this book, and to the entire BrightDot team who was patient and allowed me to focus on this project.

Thank you!

THE FOUNDATIONS
A NEW FRAMEWORK

In *Start with Heart*, I share three basic principles that too many of us in the fundraising field have either forgotten, neglected, or never learned in the first place. These concepts carry the power to transform the way you raise money.

But before we dive in, I'd like to share some hard truths that all of us in the fundraising space face today:

- Fully *93 percent of the fundraising pie* comes from major gifts.

- While high-tech analytics, wealth-screening tools, and tracking mechanisms can be useful, *they are never the catalysts* that bring in major money.

- Already strained by competing demands, *government funding for nonprofit organizations and higher education will continue to shrink* in the foreseeable future.

After years in the trenches of academia as a director of development, vice president, and college president, I now work shoulder to shoulder with leaders in nonprofit organizations and higher education to help them raise the bar of fundraising. Every day, my team and I go to work developing strategies and helping to implement them for a variety of clients from small nonprofits to major universities.

EMPATHY IS NOT AN EXTRA

I can say without equivocation that the transformation of your development office will occur when you and your staff learn to start—and stay—with heart in every facet of your work. It takes imagination, empathy, and the ability to forge a heartfelt connection to the donor to bring in a gift, especially one that is transformational in scope. While many development professionals may give lip service to this concept, too few advancement offices consciously create a culture fostering emotional intelligence. Making a fundamental shift to heart-based fundraising will send ripples throughout your office, to your board members and your donors, as well as to all the constituents and communities you serve.

When you get this part right, transformative results are bound to follow, allowing you to raise more money and impact more lives. If you've never tried the start-with-heart approach, don't berate yourself. It took me a long time—

decades—to learn and fully embrace the fundamental truths that inform it. But once I did, I came to understand that this piece is closer to the "secret sauce" for our profession than any other I know.

> I can say without equivocation that the transformation of your development office will occur when you and your staff learn to start— and stay—with heart in every facet of your work.

One episode early in my 22-year tenure as president of Georgetown College in Kentucky stands out as a personal and professional turning point, an epiphany that fundamentally reframed my thinking about how to approach major gift fundraising.

My development team and I had done extensive research about a family that was an excellent and qualified prospect for a $10 million philanthropic investment in the college. Aligned with our mission and deeply committed to the college, the family had a history of making six-figure gifts. The cherry on top: *all* of their children were alumni.

We arranged an elegant dinner at a private club for two generations of the family along with our foundation board chair, someone whom they knew and admired. The chair and I presented a detailed picture of Georgetown College—where we were and what was needed to take this sleepy college in the Bluegrass Country north of Lexington to the next level. Complete with compelling visuals and pie charts, we showed how an unrestricted gift of that size could reinvigorate—if not reinvent—the college by funding several initiatives. These included endowment funding, scholarships, and long overdue capital improvements.

The family listened attentively, posed intelligent questions and nodded approvingly. When the time was right, we made the ask.

As husband and wife departed, hand in hand, the husband said, "We'll let you know in two weeks."

The chair and I were elated, confident that success was imminent. The next day, I began drafting a press release.

Then the answer came back: No.

At first, I couldn't believe it. I rehashed the dinner, the conversation, the camaraderie and even the dessert. Nothing there. During this reflection, however, a single image kept returning: how the husband's eyes never strayed far from his wife's.

Then it dawned on me: the evening and the ask had been all about Georgetown College. Not about the family, its priorities, or what Georgetown could do for *them*. My thinking started to shift.

I knew the patriarch loved the college and trusted me. I wanted him to know that his decision didn't hurt our relationship. A series of informal, one-on-one meetings took place over the course of the next several months. This time, I made sure to ask different questions and listen deeply. He shared his deep passion to help the underprivileged, just as he had once been. I focused on what brought him joy. Flying his plane was at the top of his list, especially when he could ferry sick children to hospitals to receive special care. I watched how he cared for his employees. And there could be no doubt about how much he loved and admired his wife.

After the next few months, which brought a fundamental understanding of the man and his motivations, the time had come to offer a new proposal. I felt more in synch with him this time.

"I would like to ask you to name our new library and learning center after your wife," I said, painting a picture of what this investment would mean to his children and grandchildren, the entire Georgetown community, and especially first-generation college students. I pulled out an architectural mockup of the building in which her name was prominently featured. After my pitch, I paused, searching his eyes.

He stood quietly for a while, turning the idea over in his mind.

Then he said, "I'll do it." On the spot, he committed a seven-figure gift to name the new learning resource center after his wife.

At that moment, I internalized a profound lesson of fundraising, one that I've never forgotten: It's all about the heart. To be successful, you need to make a live connection and touch the heart of the person who can write the check, transfer the stock, and green-light the initiative.

The difference between the two meetings was simple. The first failed attempt was all about Georgetown; the second successful ask was all about the donor!

From that day forward, I coached my staff at Georgetown—and every one of my clients since—that *the institution and its needs are important but secondary*. Rule No. 1 for any ask is that the focus of your proposal be all about the donor.

> It's all about the heart. To be successful, you need to make a live connection and touch the heart of the person who can write the check, transfer the stock, and green-light the initiative.

THE BRIGHTDOT APPROACH

At BrightDot, we have developed and refined this simple but powerful approach, building upon the other-orientation of this early success story. The work begins internally, helping our clients discover or reconnect with the joy and meaning of their work. Then we move toward clarifying their "why" and that of their staff to gauge alignment with the organization and its mission. We make sure that the right people are in the right roles, and we bring this clarity of purpose and message outward to help clients grow a culture of deep connection and engaged philanthropy.

We help create environments where donors benefit from philanthropy just as much as institutions benefit from their largesse. Our clients become partners in this work, while their donors become partners in the circle of success. Everyone wins. In several cases, thanks in part to our coaching and guidance, our clients have pulled in the biggest gifts in their history.

Our approach isn't complicated but it can be a challenge to adopt for development teams schooled in more traditional, institutional-based methods. When the tools provided in this book are taken to heart, development staff and other team members become more engaged in their work, happier, and more creative, productive, and successful!

Laying the groundwork for change sets you up for success.

THE THREE PRINCIPLES

We have identified three key components for transformational change in your organization's development team that will pay dividends in the end. All revolve around emotional intelligence. When followed, they give you the ability to reconfigure your fundamental thinking about raising money. You will learn a new approach to donors, just as I did around the learning center gift for Georgetown College.

I'm not suggesting that our method will convert every "ask" into a win or that bad days will never again happen. But I am saying that by adopting these core principles, you will jumpstart a new and more effective strategy for yourself, your team, and your workplace culture, leading to greater success.

The crucial components, which I share in three main sections in the book, are:

> **No. 1. Find the joy and introduce it into the workplace.** Joy is a crucial component in the development office. Think about it: philanthropy is voluntary. Donors may put up with a disagreeable power company representative (after all, everyone needs to keep the lights on), but nothing compels them to interact with you. Inner light, joy, and authentic

engagement need to emanate from development officers so that donors want to be with you.

No. 2. Create messages that connect, and share that sense of what matters—along with the institutional "why"—with every team member, who serves as a conduit to the stories that bring life to you and your institution. When development directors are living their "why," they are living joyfully, and are poised to be top performers.

No. 3. Tap the power of emotional intelligence and interpersonal connection to recast the way you interact with constituents, donors, and each other. Learning to cultivate and tap into your emotional intelligence will raise you to the next level.

Focusing on these three components will change the culture inside your office. When coupled with setting big, hairy, audacious goals (or BHAGs, with thanks to Jim Collins), you set the stage for transforming your organization with bold ambitions and benchmarks. Donors admire courage and vision and will vote with their pocketbooks.

Each main section—or principle—provides stories and anecdotes that illustrate the methods we recommend along with tips to help implement them, data to back up our methods, and takeaway material.

Once you have read this book, it is my wish that you will see how the human side of fundraising, accessed through the intentional creation of joy; the identification of authentic messages; and tapping into the power of emotional intelligence fuels groundbreaking gift-giving. Let's get started!

But first, we need to look at the elephant in the room: what's getting in our way.

THE REALITIES
THE HARD WORK OF HEART

My career in fundraising began back in 1982 when I landed the job of Director of Corporate and Foundation Giving for Gardner-Webb University in Boiling Springs, North Carolina. I was 28 years old, with a newly minted doctorate and brimming with "I can change the world!" enthusiasm and ambition. Even then, I had set my sights on becoming a college president. It was a stroke of luck to land an interview with Gardner-Webb's dynamic president, Dr. Craven E. Williams, and forge an immediate connection.

"I can teach you everything I know," he said, "and some things I don't!"

Dr. Williams had been at the helm of Gardner-Webb just a few years. His confidence was infectious, and he eagerly took this even-younger whippersnapper under wing. Working as his sidekick (and driver for our long trips around the Carolinas), I had the opportunity to watch him interacting with board members, faculty, staff, and students. His generous but authoritative approach was effective, and I took note. From Dr. Williams, I learned all the fundamentals: how to cultivate relationships; how to identify projects for funding; and how and when to make the ask.

Contrary to the image of top administrators indulging in fine dining on the college expense account, my hard-charging boss was singularly focused on success, refusing to stop for meals as we hit the road to meet benefactors, prospects, and alumni. To tame growling stomachs, after one meeting while off to the next, he'd whip out his granola-like stash of peanuts, M&M's, and raisins, pour me a handful, then help himself.

Of course, the fundraising landscape has changed dramatically since then. Back then, the majority of donors gave at three junctures in the year: commencement, class reunions, and year-end. Major gifts and legacy giving were on the radar but the approach was haphazard, even capricious. Today, those who wish to excel—or even just stay in the game—must broaden their skill set while sharpening the ones they have.

DISRUPTION IS THE NEW NORMAL

In recent years, almost every modern industry and profession has been disrupted by accelerating change and has had to take a measure of itself and recalibrate. "Uber upended the taxi business while Airbnb did the same to the hotel industry; brick-and-mortar retail is reinventing itself to hold its own against exploding internet sales," my colleague Wanda Urbanska wrote in one of our blogs. As she explained:

> The development field is no exception. Entitlement fundraising—in which respected nonprofit professionals simply do good work and interface with donors (often only reluctantly) through such tried-and-true methods as annual appeals and galas, expecting money to continue to stream in—is simply no longer sufficient to get the job done, much less to scale the work.
>
> Ironically, for years, too many fundraising professionals have viewed their work almost as a necessary evil, with development officers playing the part of supplicants on bended knee. Only when fundraisers shift from a transactional, sales mindset—in which the donor is the "score" rather than a partner in philanthropy—to a transformative one will they gain mastery of the field. Once development officers bring donors and potential donors into the fold of authentic relationship, offering up financial participation as an opportunity for personal growth and a way to express values, they will be aligned for large success.

Once this paradigm shift has been made, fundraising can become "sacred work," write Jennifer McCrea and Jeffrey C. Walker in their landmark 2013 book *The Generosity Network: New Transformational Tools for Successful Fund-Raising,* "a beautiful practice characterized by compassion, joy, commitment and partnership."

> Only when fundraisers shift from a transactional, sales mindset, in which the donor is the "score" rather than a partner in philanthropy, to a transformative one will they gain mastery of the field.

SOBERING FUNDRAISING REALITIES

There are sobering realities that development officers—and their teams and leaders—need to recognize, reckon with, and respond to as they adapt to shifting sands.

For example, in the field of higher education, many are questioning whether a private liberal arts education is worth the price tag. In 2019, the Bill & Melinda Gates Foundation decided to study the issue. Sue Desmond-Hellmann, CEO of the Gates Foundation, told *University World News,* "As the cost of a credential rises and student debt goes to record levels, people are actually asking a question I never thought I'd hear, 'Is going to college a reliable path to economic opportunity?'"

I am and always will be a proponent of a college education—and in particular a comprehensive, liberal arts education—for any capable student. Having an educated population contributes greatly to our common good and welfare as a nation, much as it contributes to the enhancement of those individuals who achieve it.

As my colleague Dr. Richard E. Sours, past president of Iowa's William Penn University, wrote recently, "by virtue of earning a college degree, the graduate will be looked upon as a family and community leader, and possibly a state or national leader. The knowledge base, life skills, level of social awareness and respect, and their strong moral and ethical character should be evident and should serve them throughout their lives. These attributes may, or may not, lead to economic opportunity, but that is secondary to their ability to 'see more' throughout their lifetime."

What is more, a recent Georgetown University study shows that college graduates earn on average $1 million dollars more than high school graduates over a lifetime. To that end, one of our nonprofit clients is diligently working to level the playing field for underserved populations. The Baby Bundle initiative at the United Way of Coastal Fairfield County (UWCFC) seeks to move the hearts of donors by asking them to invest in the nurturing of at-risk babies from birth to age three. This prepares children for educational opportunities. Our colleagues at UWCFC know that without this investment only one out of ten of these babies will go on to college. Private funding for mental health and collective impact issues such as this one become more vitally needed as governmental funding continues to shrink.

THE NEED FOR MAJOR DONORS

In the world of higher education and in fact at all nonprofits, the reliance on major gifts has been accelerated by the rapid rise in income inequality in America, with more money in the hands of a very few—namely, the rich and super rich.

The pressure to bring in more funding from top donors has been exacerbated by the change in the tax code which took effect in 2018. The Tax Cuts and Jobs Act of 2017 boosted the standard deduction on income taxes from $6,350 in 2017 to $12,000 for single people and from $12,700 to $24,00 for married people filing jointly. The impact on middle- to upper-income tax payers is significant in disincentivizing them from giving to nonprofits, including educational institutions.

However, a 2018 report in *MarketWatch*, citing a U.S. Trust study on high-net worth philanthropy, shows that "the wealthy are least likely to change their habits. A majority of wealthy donors said they expect to maintain their giving levels (84 percent) and another 4 percent said they intend to increase that amount in 2018, regardless the new tax law."

No doubt about it, development officers must work overtime to reinvent themselves and set themselves up for professional and institutional success with the all-important, deep-pocketed major donor. Developing the skill set to make meaningful connections with this group is what every major gift officer must do. It is also at the center of what we teach.

> A majority of wealthy donors said they expect to maintain their giving levels (84 percent) and another 4 percent said they intend to increase that amount in 2018, regardless the new tax law.

FACTORS INHIBITING TOP PERFORMANCE IN FUNDRAISERS

Throughout my career, both in academia and later in my work with nonprofit clients, I've observed several recurring factors that inhibit top performance in fundraising. These represent obstacles to success for individuals and institutions. Three major factors include:

Fear: Especially over the past several years, I've witnessed an increasing atmosphere of fear and distrust among development officers, college staff, and, in some cases, donors themselves. Too often, the spirit of hope, adventure, potential, and renewal—which fuel creativity, growth, and generosity—has been displaced by negativity, cynicism and fear. Individuals awash in fear rarely make effective fundraisers, any more than such individuals attract friends, neighbors, or romantic partners. Fear repels; optimism attracts!

Turnover: Another issue facing many development teams is the reality of 18-month turnover. Studies show that this is how long the average fundraiser stays in their position. This staff churn can be deadly for a college development or alumni office, which banks on institutional memory and the building of relationships to keep it alive and kicking. This short-term tenure is most often attributable to development professionals believing that they are not thriving in their jobs. A recent study published by *the Chronicle of Philanthropy* indicates that up to 51 percent of all development professionals are considering leaving the profession in the next two years. In many cases, their bosses don't grant them enough time, training, or connections to get their sea legs on the job. In other cases, if they *are* performing well, the word spreads, and they're poached by the competition.

Silos: All too often the annual fund manager is not speaking to the major gifts officer who is not sharing information—or challenges—with the vice president for Institutional Advancement or anyone else on the team. What is more, when development and alumni offices in a college or university reach a certain size, there's a strong danger of silos and turf wars springing up, working against institutional best interests. Indeed, at all nonprofits over the years, I've seen countless examples where uncoachable clients insist on doing things "their way." This allows them to stay in their comfort zone, while inhibiting the chance for top performance. Too many silos and not enough bridges invariably spell missed opportunities and bring disappointing results.

In any development office, when you see a combination of rapid staff turnover and a fearful, backbiting culture characterized by individual and departmental silos, and when you witness a lack of personal and institutional accountability, the red flags are flying high. Such distress signals call for cultural assessment, intervention, and change. Of course, turning a wayward ship midcourse is never easy, but once you acknowledge the situation, you can then go to work to get yourself back on track. So how do you counter these draining and all-too-common tendencies and habits and reboot your advancement operation?

> When you see a combination of rapid staff
> turnover and, a fearful, backbiting culture
> characterized by individual and departmental
> silos, and when you witness a lack of personal
> and institutional accountability, the red flags
> are flying high. Such distress signals call for
> cultural assessment, intervention, and change.

A QUESTION OF CULTURE

At BrightDot, we've learned that the tools of emotional intelligence can be readily applied in the fundraising space. Tapping into the human side of fundraising launches the hard work of heart in a myriad of ways—not only with donors but at the individual level, in the team space, and when cultivating institutional partners.

In our next section—Principle #1—we will delve into the potent power of joy to kickstart the process of cultural change.

PRINCIPLE #1
FIND THE JOY

There can be no joy in living
without joy in work.
—*Thomas Aquinas*

The gift of reading given to me by my mother in childhood has continued to pay dividends, blessing my own long and happy marriage. Jan and I often read books together. One of the most meaningful books we've discussed recently is C.S. Lewis's 1955 autobiography, *Surprised by Joy: The Shape of My Early Life.* As Jan and I contemplated the concept of joy, we came to understand that it is a distinct emotion—different from pleasure (fleeting), different from happiness (a state of being). Joy is ineffable and inscrutable. You can set the stage for it but you can never predict when it will come, or hold onto it once it's there. Joy surprises in magical, unexpected moments.

"(Joy) has a lithe, muscular lightness to it," Lewis writes. "It dashes in with the agility of a hummingbird claiming its nectar from the flower, and ... then vanishes, leaving a wake of mystery and longing behind it."

For Jan and me, joy is the July arrival of the first fig from our tree in the side yard or reading the part of our son's Christmas letter where our seven-year-old granddaughter announces her "greatest wish" this year is to rid the world of plastic straws.

JOY AT WORK: AN OXYMORON?

Why do the words of C.S. Lewis speak to me so strongly, driving my passion to help colleges, universities, and nonprofits of every stripe raise more money? What, you might ask, does joy have to do with our work? The answer is *everything*.

While the hard-nosed advancement skeptic may argue that their organization needs to raise money to stay in business and that they have no time for fluff—i.e., extras like creating a joyful workplace—I maintain that fostering joy in the workplace is integral to the process and should rise to the level of a strategic workplace imperative in every development office.

In fact, one of the key concepts we impart to clients is that establishing a culture of joy at work is nothing short of essential for success. When individuals are filled with joy in a workplace they love, they set themselves up for high performance. *Joy at work can change everything—including your bottom line!*

> When individuals are filled with joy in a workplace they love, they set themselves up for high performance. Joy at work can change everything—including your bottom line!

When you read about the results of the recent comprehensive campaign at Meredith College, an elite women's college in Raleigh, North Carolina, you'll see how joy expresses itself in the culture of the workplace and how it leads to remarkable outcomes.

THE MEREDITH COLLEGE MIRACLE

If you listen to the doubters, there's never really a "good" time to launch a major, multiyear comprehensive campaign. The argument against it is predictable: donor fatigue has set in. These are challenging times in the world of higher education. For private colleges. For women's colleges. The economy could be better. Or if the economy is soaring, people are worried that the next downturn is just around the corner. The list of excuses goes on.

Founded in 1891, Meredith College has been a stalwart in female education in the South for generations and consistently ranks in the top 20 percent of American colleges by Forbes.com. Now attracting students from all over the country and world, the college has many points of pride including postgraduation employment and graduate school placement numbers well above 90 percent along with a loyal, tight-knit alumni base.

Within a year after taking over the helm of Meredith College, Dr. Jo Allen bit the bullet and launched an ambitious comprehensive campaign. The year was 2012, and the economy was just clambering out of its worst downturn since the Great Depression. A 1980 Meredith graduate, President Allen announced that this campaign would be Meredith's biggest and most successful ever. The stretch goal for the campaign—called Beyond Strong— was set at $75 million, nail-bitingly aggressive given that Meredith's endowment at the time was sitting right at $67 million.

Yet Meredith's gamble paid off. Following the soft launch in July 2012, in just over six years to the finish line in December 2018, the campaign closed the books at over $90 million raised—surpassing its goal by a whopping 20 percent! As a result, its endowment grew to $116 million, nearly doubling in size. Our firm was privileged to be engaged by Meredith for one component of its comprehensive campaign (more on our firm's contribution in Principle #3).

So how did the master strategists at Meredith College pull off this remarkable feat?

Inspired by joy

After standard campaign start-up steps such as hiring CapDev, a well-respected consulting firm, to create a feasibility study, articulating big-picture objectives and determining a dollar goal, theme, and timeline, Allen turned her attention to the "softer stuff" inside Johnson Hall.

Having recently left a high-functioning team at Widener University in Chester, Pennsylvania, where she had served as senior vice president and provost, Allen had the opportunity to observe the crucial elements needed to build collegiality. Her boss and mentor there was former President Jim Harris, who possessed deep development experience and was skilled at cementing the team bonds and trust necessary for success.

Though impressed by Meredith College's existing Institutional Advancement leadership team, Allen understood that to make the campaign work, she needed to build deep trust inside the team, to demonstrate that she was "all in" and to introduce some outside-the-box thinking.

"I start with the idea that all work ought to have some fun to it," she says. "If it's never fun—always *work*—it doesn't interest me at all," she says. In fact, what would turn out to be the campaign's signature joy-stirring ritual began quite by accident.

Tuesdays with the president

While still in the early planning stages of the campaign, President Allen called a meeting with her two top lieutenants, Lennie Barton, vice president for institutional advancement, and Cindy Godwin, associate vice president for advancement. To get away from the bustle, buzz, and phones of the president's office, Allen decided to hold the meeting at Massey House, her elegant residence on campus. There, the trio found "quiet space," getting comfortable in overstuffed chairs.

That initial session proved so productive that when exiting the meeting, everyone had the same idea. "We all had a mutual ah-ha moment that we should continue to meet at the house," she says.

Thus, the "Tuesdays with the President" tradition was born.

Getting down to business

As regular as a weekly Rotary Club meeting, the sessions took place every Tuesday afternoon at 4. Everyone was expected to be fully present. To set the stage for relaxed sharing and creative brainstorming, libations—usually wine, as well as standard-fare tea, lemonade, and soft drinks—were laid out along with a plate of cheese and crackers. Occasionally, leftover fare from a reception the night before would appear.

Godwin recalls looking forward to the Tuesday meetings, even dressing more casually than usual when she had no off-campus calls that day. When he arrived, Barton would loosen—or take off—his tie.

"At least one of us…okay, it's me," jokes President Allen, "could kick off her shoes!"

After a few sips and a few jokes, the brain trust would get down to business. Part strategic-planning session, part debriefing of the week before and part priority-setting for the upcoming week, the meetings followed a regular rhythm. Each person would provide an update. Kim McCall Whitley, the campaign coordinator, generally sat in to take notes, which she distributed the following morning in the form of to-do lists.

"Everyone's favorite was giving me a to-do list," Allen puts in. The team was expected to jump on their tasks immediately if not sooner—making phone calls, writing thank you notes, scheduling visits, compiling event guest lists, and drafting proposals.

Though the core team was always present, marketing people and Major Gift Officers (MGOs) with big news or big questions would cycle in.

"When one of our MGOs landed a $5 million gift, she was invited," says Allen. The president remembers pulling out all the stops and celebrating that feat by crowning the MGO with an over-the-top tiara, then uncorking a bottle of champagne. "It was a fun, spur-of-the-moment thing!"

"I loved Tuesdays with the president and looked forward to each one," says Godwin. "It was a safe place to strategize with permission to disagree. The operative words were *fun, productive, strategic, supportive.* That is why we have continued them beyond the campaign."

Too often institutional development offices' presidents and executive directors hold development at arm's length, preferring to act as aloof figureheads for a campaign. They will show up for major meetings, deliver remarks at events, and pose for photo ops, but leave the strategy and minutiae of raising money to others. Jo Allen's decision to roll up her sleeves and get in the trenches with the rest of the team made all the difference.

"Having President Allen devote so much time to our campaign—and with such generosity of spirit—was critical to our success," says Barton, who, before joining Meredith in 2010, had a decades-long career in alumni relations at nearby North Carolina State University. "Quite frankly, I've never seen anything like her commitment to the Tuesday meetings, either in spirit or in regularity."

> Too often institutional development offices' presidents and executive directors hold development at arm's length, preferring to act as aloof figureheads for a campaign.... [Getting] in the trenches with the rest of the team [makes] all the difference.

Observing donors with the acuity of Jane Austen

A published author and gifted writer, Allen set the tone for the meetings. Her focus on observing the passing scene proved to be a major development asset. Allen challenged the team to tap such traditionally "feminine" skills as keen observation and intuition in probing the personalities and preferences of donors and prospects. The activity was at once deadly serious business and fun sport.

To that end, each team member would have their turn deconstructing interactions with donors and providing updates or piling nuance onto previous understandings. With the acuity of Jane Austen, the team found no offhand comment or tidbit too trivial for scrutiny. For instance, a toss-away comment a donor might be heard making (i.e., "Barbecue is overrated!" or "Why aren't there more statues of women in public places?") when shared with

Godwin or Barton, would be added to the big picture, and often entered into the donor's profile. In addition to the requisite business alliances and fallouts, social and familial connections, the trio unpacked political leanings, pet peeves, and even what Allen calls "peculiarities" to gain a fuller understanding of the person.

"Let me tell you," Barton says, "what's said in Vegas stays in Vegas."

The sessions, week after week, took on the tenor of an unfolding stage play in real time, including dramatic turns, announcements, disappointments, and the arrival of an unexpected donor or the disappearance of a once-hot prospect. On occasion, Allen says, play-acting became a part of the mix in figuring ways to deal with such challenges as persnickety donors or ones loathe to show their cards. More than once, the group shared ideas for "gracefully redirecting" interminable discussion about dogs, ailments, and vacations to move to the business at hand: a donor's investment in Meredith College.

"We were just having so much fun," Godwin recalls. "Still are!" Indeed, because the sessions worked so well during the course of the six-year campaign, Allen decided to continue the meetings to keep the momentum going.

Taking her cues from President Allen, Cindy Godwin recalls that as the campaign was revving up, she developed her own joy-spreading protocols with her advancement staff of nine. In the early months and first year of the campaign, she recalls, "before we raised so many $1 million gifts, we made a very big deal out of each one." Godwin recalls special congratulatory banners being created and unfurled inside Johnson Hall, so that no one could miss the news. A big fuss was made at staff meetings about every major victory. Indeed, there can be no doubt that such acknowledgment and heartfelt appreciation goes farther for most employees than monetary bonuses alone. They touch the heart.

LESSONS FROM MEREDITH COLLEGE

When aggregated, the steps Meredith College followed seamlessly built joy, culture, and a supportive in-house structure. I remain impressed by the combination of care and smart management Cindy Godwin brings to her team. Implementing these seven practices will bear fruit for you, too. They are:

1. **Talk regularly** (usually daily) with staff

2. **Hold weekly meetings** where everyone has a chance to discuss strategy and compare notes

3. **Say thank you** a lot

4. **Laugh and cry** together

5. **Share goals** with the entire staff—no secrets

6. **Give perks** to fit the person (for example, for every $1 million gift, female staffers are given a day spa treatment, while men receive a gift certificate to an exclusive restaurant)

7. **Divvy up "fun" assignments**, like staffing an alumnae trip abroad so everyone has their turn!

Joy builds trust; trust builds joy

What happened inside the advancement office at Meredith—joy created with intention—catalyzed into a magical spirit that carried the day. The team bonded, celebrated, and felt that they were rowing together in the pursuit of a north star they all had sight of. For every win, the entire team took credit. For every loss, everyone on the team paused to mourn.

The joy campaign built trust and cohesion. "If you don't have trust," says Allen, "you're in the blame game. Then it's, 'Who's getting the credit for a win?' Or, 'Who's taking blame for what didn't materialize?'" That kind of spirit, she says, is neither fun nor productive.

> What happened inside the advancement office at Meredith—joy created with intention—catalyzed into a magical spirit that carried the day.... The joy campaign built of trust and cohesion. "If you don't have trust," says Allen, "you're in the blame game."

CREATING WORKPLACE RITUALS

When I reflect upon such successes as the Meredith campaign and many others, invariably I see that there are universal practices and truths from which we can all learn. One recurrent aspect of the successful construction of a joyful workplace is the creation and steady use of ritual.

As you've seen, the team at Meredith consciously crafted rituals for both leadership and rank and file in their office. These rituals served to increase employee engagement, thus elevating the mood and performance of the entire team. Take stock of your own rituals. How many nonwork get-togethers does your staff have? If you only gather once a year for a holiday party, that's not cutting it. While you may worry that intentionally creating in-house rituals is contrived, costly, and distracts you from the business of raising money, nothing could be further from the truth. In fact, bringing your staff together is one of the best investments you can make.

> While you may worry that intentionally creating in-house rituals is contrived, costly, and distracts you from the business of raising money, nothing could be further from the truth. In fact, bringing your staff together is one of the best investments you can make.

The beauty of initiating new rituals is that you can get creative and dream up fun new ideas that suit your personality and that of your staff. One of our esteemed clients, Ara Serjoie, vice president for advancement at Guilford College in Greensboro, North Carolina, introduced a Monday morning ritual that gets the staff off on the right foot each week. You may have guessed that, yes, it involves food. Most every Monday, Serjoie brings in home-baked goods (often his own creations), fruit, or some other special treat for the team to enjoy.

"Mondays have a lot of potential," he says, "and this ritual helps the team feel welcomed back, energized, and ready to start off the week on a happy note. It also reminds them that I appreciate them and their efforts." Typically, on Monday afternoons, the entire staff gathers for a half-hour coffee break where everyone chats informally. Occasionally, team members use the time to conduct peer-to-peer training or have a conversation around a key topic.

Rituals need to happen regularly and have predictable elements. Food is always a good starting point. Weekly or biweekly meetings are ideal. *But at minimum, you need to schedule monthly meetings to bring staff together to gin up camaraderie and fun.*

Create some predictability around your ritual by holding it the second and fourth Wednesdays of each month, for instance, and giving it a goofy name, such as *Wild Wednesdays!* You could host a monthly "lunch-and-learn" event, in which guest speakers are brought in, lunch is provided, and other team-building elements are in place. For example, a different staffer could give a five-minute profile at each meeting. When I was a member of the Rotary Club, I always enjoyed the member profile presentations the most as they provided a window into the fascinating people right under your nose. Take photos and post on Facebook, Twitter, and Instagram. Everyone feels good and your team feels validated. You get the idea!

If your budget can accommodate buying the lunches, offer your team a treat. I've had board members fund regular lunch meetings (and occasionally join to break bread). Or you can organize a "brown bag" lunch asking everyone to bring in their own fare. The important thing is to *do it regularly, without fail, and with predictable elements.* I guarantee that wonderful surprises are sure to ensue. Never forget that ritual works because it gets people together, talking, eating, and sharing experience. Regular, face-to-face meetings are at once the glue that creates community and the substance that holds it together.

FIVE BUILDING BLOCKS OF JOY

Ritual is crucial, but it's not the only component to move the culture needle in your office. I'd like to share five basic building blocks of joy that will help augment ritual and create positive energy, setting the stage for success.

1. Recognize milestones

Whether a major gift has closed, or whether a goal is met (or surpassed), identify a way to celebrate. If your office is into goofy tricks, you could put up a reusable foam trellis around the honoree's doorway or desk.

The same goes for staff members' birthdays or anniversaries. Remember to take time to acknowledge and celebrate these big moments in their lives. You can do it with silly hats or by ordering in fruit salad or a special cupcake. If you have the budget, bring in a mariachi band! Again, leaving a little gift with a card—even a $25 gift certificate to the local coffee shop or a pair of movie tickets—will mean a lot. These gestures go a long way in the creation of joy at work.

Such remembrances will also remind your staff to appropriately steward donors (i.e., never forget someone's birthday!). If you can give a nod to your institution in the process, so much the better. At Guilford College, Ara

Serjoie and his team use original student art birthday cards and greeting cards. Benefactors, faculty, and staff all get a printed card signed by every member of the team. (And, to cover all the bases, every recipient with an email receives an electronic version as well!)

Whether internally with your team or externally with your donors and other constituents, look inside your campus or nonprofit for resources to tap. Guilford has an on-campus organic farm, and the development office frequently procures holiday, wedding, and new baby gifts from it.

2. Create staff-only celebrations

As with staff-only rituals, host staff-only celebrations. Come up with a theme—Mardi Gras, Cinco de Mayo, Halloween—and pull out all the stops! Internal celebrations are money well spent because they reinforce how valued your team is. At Meredith, Jo Allen created a NASA space rocket party to kick off the comprehensive campaign in 2012 and used the same theme (and even the same papier-mâché NASA space rocket) to celebrate its completion eight years later. A large cooler was stocked with red, white, and blue ice cream rockets to fit the theme of take-off. "To create magic, you need to incorporate an element of surprise," Allen says. Even adults in dignified settings need to occasionally unleash their inner child!

3. Offer praise

Social lubricants, like praise and friendly greetings, brighten the day and do their part to brighten office culture. One of our clients, a supervisor in a community college development office, realized that she didn't enjoy hearing praise herself; in fact, it made her uncomfortable. As a result of her own praise-phobia, she had never fully understood how many of her staff craved uplifting words and positive feedback, not only at annual review but regularly. Once she got this, she went out of her way to offer praise to her staff, whether through a positive email, text, or word in the hall. She soon noticed that even a few words of encouragement made a big difference on morale.

4. The Attitude of Gratitude

Cicero's wisdom about gratitude being "the greatest of virtues" and "the parent of all the others" is on target. You can build a culture of gratitude in your office by reminding yourself and your team about all the things, large and small, for which you are grateful. It starts with the small stuff.

"Thank you for refilling the copier," is something you don't *have* to say but when you do, others reciprocate with similar expressions of gratitude. Never forget that attitude and language are fundamental building blocks of a joy- and respect-based office culture. They set a high bar of expectation and atmosphere for your office.

> "Gratitude is not only the greatest of virtues, but the parent of all the others."
> —Marcus Tullius Cicero

5. *Leading with joy*

Having a joyful leader will help enormously in creating a culture of joy in your office. One of my star students at Georgetown College, Shelley Prevost (who also served on our BrightDot team), once held the job of Director of Happiness at a for-profit company in Chattanooga, Tennessee. In that capacity, she engaged, supported, counseled, and applauded employees. She commiserated when they were stressed, going through boxes of tissue. Each of these components of employee engagement is important for every leader to adopt. When the person at the top models this empathetic approach—seeing the promotion of happiness and joy as an essential part of their job—joy will spread rapidly throughout the culture of your office!

Once these joy-stirring methods have permeated your organization, moments of connection and feelings of contentment among staffers will become the norm (rather than the exception). These feelings will spill over into in-person meetings with prospects and donors. And they will even impact the tone of voiceprints during phone calls and the spirit of letters, emails, and texts your development officers send. (See Principle #2. Create Messages That Connect.) But more than anything, it will make you and your staff *want* to come into work the next day and make a difference in the lives of the people you serve.

DONORS WANT TO FEEL JOY, TOO

Never forget that your donors and prospects are human, too. They can sniff out contrived compliments, false modesty and anything resembling transactional interactions. They respond to genuine emotion, enthusiasm, and commitment. When joy is in the room, donors want some, too! And when they feel joy—and when their gift is the right fit—you will feel it, too!

I'll never forget Rollie and Lena Graves, Georgetown College Ambassadors whose countenances were filled with joy. Early in my presidency, I was approached by Rollie Graves who pledged an annual $10,000 gift for me as president to use at my discretion in helping students in need prepare for the job market.

Each year, I had the pleasure of selecting worthy students and investing in them through the Graves Fund. Such things as greenlighting the purchase of interview clothing, covering travel expenses to job interviews, and paying for pre-professional training programs off campus were typical allocations.

After the fact, I'd make a point of introducing the recipients to the Graveses. The students were invariably thrilled to meet their benefactors, and the Graves were equally delighted to meet these ambitious youngsters who had been born with plastic (rather than silver) spoons in their mouths. Rollie Graves had always been for the underdog. While the couple never had grandchildren, they experienced joy through their surrogate grandchildren, some of Georgetown's neediest students. As a result, lasting relationships were developed.

And here's another delightful outcome of the creation of the Graves Fund: it led to a six-figure estate gift for the college!

LET JOY DO THE WORK

Returning to the subject of C.S. Lewis's definition of joy—it is ineffable and fleeting. Remember, you can't hold onto joy. But you can set the stage for it. By consciously fostering a culture of joy and *joie de vivre* in your team, you will make these moments happen more often.

As we've explored when unpacking the Meredith College comprehensive campaign and learned how the introduction of joy into the process worked miracles for them, we also saw how the infectious nature of joy expresses itself. It starts at the top, trickles down to the rank-and-file on the advancement team, radiates around the campus and to alumnae and then to the larger Meredith community, before closing the loop by trickling back up the chain of command.

As a result, gifts come in, then more gifts. Before you know it, even the *donors* have assumed the role of development officers, as they work overtime to bring in gifts from within their circles, or open the doors for you to secure gifts. Suddenly, you're all on a train to which everyone wants a ticket, like an invitation to a coveted party.

Of course, we recommend a number of customized strategies to clients as they work to transform their office culture, important items covered in the following sections of the book. There are hard skills, such as understanding financial information to determine the capacity of individuals to give, and understanding the vehicles for doing so, such as trusts and annuities. MGOs will need to know how to craft messages and stories that speak to your mission, as well as how to tap into the power of emotional intelligence. But, in every case, we recommend starting with heart, and starting with joy!

A BRIGHTDOT QUESTION:
"Your Favorite Childhood Toy"

In our work with clients, we've developed a question that has the capacity to transport them to another time and place. The place is childhood, and more often than not, the answer to this question conjures up joy. We have found that this question works for us nine times out of ten.

When you are out on the road, meeting prospects and donors, trying to understand them, what makes them tick, their pains, sorrows, and interests, sometimes you get stuck. If you're trying to draw someone out and having difficulty, try this question out.

Donor Question: *What was your favorite childhood toy?*

Let me give you an example of how it worked for me. When I recently called on Baylor University in Waco, Texas, I met a high-level member of the advancement team. She seemed closed to the concept of what BrightDot was offering— emotional intelligence training for her team that would result in higher performance. There I was, sitting in this senior leader's office, trying to make the case that our work could help their team gain cohesion and excitement, and ultimately raise more money.

Her body language told me that she wanted our meeting to conclude, so she could move onto other matters.

Then I laid it on her. "What was your favorite childhood toy?"

She looked at me, puzzled, then paused to think.

"I can't think of a toy exactly, but I do know that when the ice cream truck drove through our neighborhood in the summer, it was always the highlight of my day."

At the airport, heading back home, I went online and ordered a miniature metal ice cream truck and had it sent to her.

I didn't hear anything from her for about a month. Then I got a short note from her. It read, "Damn, you're good."

This toy opened a closed door and gave me insight to this woman's childhood and joy. This is the power of this question. Ultimately, we *did* win a contract with Baylor's George W. Truett Theological Seminary. Asking just one powerful question forged a special connection, one that I share with all of you.

Try it sometime.

CREATE MESSAGES THAT CONNECT

*"No story lives unless someone wants to listen.
The stories we love best do live in us forever."*
—*J.K. Rowling*

Back in 1991, the opportunity of a lifetime presented itself. At age 39, I was invited to interview to be president of Georgetown College in Kentucky. The position represented the fulfillment of a dream and an ambition I'd been pursuing for over a decade.

Of course, I wore an appropriate suit, was clean-shaven, and my shoes were buffed to a sheen. But looking back on that momentous interview now, I see that it all came down to messaging. What mattered most was how I expressed myself, the messages I chose to convey, and the way in which they were delivered.

THE POWER OF AN AUTHENTIC MESSAGE

Though Simon Sinek hadn't yet popularized his "know your why" terminology back then, I intuited that a winning expression of my "why"—why I wanted to take the helm of Georgetown College and what I could uniquely bring to the institution—could prove to be the deal maker... or breaker.

After a lively and positive exchange with the board of directors about my background growing up in North Carolina and Mississippi, being the son of a Baptist minister, my philosophy of education, and my ideas about what was needed to move this sleepy Southern college into the 21st century, one of the board members tossed out a closing question, almost a throwaway: "Is there anything else that we need to know about you?"

I swallowed hard. "Yes," I started, "and it's one of the reasons you need to hire me. I've had an experience that will allow me to relate to 50 percent of the population. Because of what happened to me—something that knocked me to my knees—I am no longer afraid of failure." I paused: "I've been divorced."

Everyone around the table grew quiet. You could just feel the wheels spinning. While even 30 years ago divorce was common in America, the conservative Kentucky Baptist Convention—of which Georgetown College was a member—held tight to traditional values. Going in, I knew that the college had never before hired a divorced president.

A female board member finally broke the silence by saying, "I'm the mother of two divorced children," she said. "I don't see any reason we should not consider your candidacy." Others began nodding in agreement. A second round of interviews followed, then the offer.

Once hired, I embarked on a steep learning curve, one encompassing the challenges of running a religiously affiliated liberal arts school in a time of rising secularism; the difficulty of recruiting and retaining gifted students, athletes, faculty, and staff; and the growing importance of fundraising for a college president.

But what allowed me the opportunity for my 22-year journey at Georgetown College? So much of it came down to messaging, positioning, and storytelling. I had to flip the black mark of my divorce and weave it into a paradigm-shifting narrative suggesting that that experience could actually *help* the college prepare for the future.

What I learned then and have had reinforced many times since is that getting the messaging right can change the trajectory of a conversation or opportunity. I'm not going to suggest that my messaging has always been on target or that my every at bat has resulted in a home run, or even a base hit. Far from it. I have taken my lumps like the next guy. But I do know this: the right messaging—

crafted in advance of a meeting—makes all the difference in getting the job, the grant, the gift, or the new person you want to hire.

I do know this: the right messaging—crafted in advance of a meeting—makes all the difference in getting the job, the grant, the gift, or the new person you want to hire.

In this section, I will provide key concepts, and share valuable and proven tools, for helping you develop effective messages. You can think of those messages as starting with you, as an individual, extending out to your team, and then rippling beyond. Following are the elements to guide your thinking:

- Developing and sustaining a culture of storytelling
- Getting to your individual and organizational "Why"
- Telling your story with heart and confidence
- Staying true to your own guiding principles
- Applying your stories to your donor-facing messaging
- Always saying "thank you"

A NEW MANDATE FOR STORYTELLING

Just as creating joy in your office is essential for success, the creation of authentic and engaging content stands in the first tier of needs for your organization, both in the building of culture and the raising of money. Magic happens when our clients find "sticky messaging"—that is, words, themes, and stories that are moving and stay with you. I have seen the faces of clients light up the moment they hear messages expressed properly. And I have seen donors pick up their checkbooks, sign pledge cards, or click on their smartphones to transfer money upon hearing a moving, appropriately worded appeal.

Identifying and developing authentic messaging begins with each member of your team finding meaning in stories that matter to them individually and that connect them deeply to their work. Their personal stories forge a vibrant live wire to your organizational mission.

In my decades of fundraising, I have learned that without individual and internal stories, it is virtually impossible for employees to make the necessary connection to the larger mission. If they describe your organization and its needs without the animating connections that bring their messages to life, they come off like the proverbial limp handshake. It doesn't work, it rarely takes, and often amounts to a door-shuttering donor turn-off. Identifying your own story—and conflating it with that of your institution—is critical to engaging donors and ensuring successful outcomes.

A CULTURE OF STORYTELLING

In order to tap the power of story where you work, the first order of business is to *consciously create a culture of storytelling* inside your office. Storytelling is a powerful tool for helping staff members identify their personal "why" (more on that shortly) and forge a deep connection to their work. Let me demonstrate the power of harnessing personal story with one of our clients, a frontline community college fundraiser.

"I love my work," Roxanne Miller, director of development for the Wake Tech Foundation, told Wanda Urbanska, a member of our team who was providing coaching and message development guidance. "It's hard for me to imagine working anywhere else."

During one coaching session, Urbanska challenged Miller to dig into her past for personal stories to help explain the close connection she feels to Wake Technical Community College, North Carolina's largest, with some 70,000 students spread over nine campuses. Wanda knew that when Miller identified a deeper, emotional "why" to her work as a fundraiser, it would immediately deepen her already-successful connection to her work on behalf of students in need.

At their next session, Miller handed in a sheet with several stories she'd put to paper. She then told them from her heart. One story was so powerful, Urbanska had to hold back tears.

ROXANNE'S STORY:
"The Little Hand Up Needed"

When Miller was just three years old, her father took off, leaving her 21-year-old mother to fend for the little girl and her baby sister. It was a struggle for the young mother, who had no college education or marketable skill, to figure out how to care for her daughters, pay the bills, and put food on the table. Winter was fast approaching in Tenants Harbor, Maine, and a power company agent had been dispatched to disconnect the service for nonpayment. Upon arrival, he learned of their dire straits. What the man did next has entered into Miller family lore.

Instead of cutting off the power, he returned to his office and paid the bill out of his own pocket. Miller's mother still describes this gift—that might seem minor to some—as "the little hand up I needed to get on my feet." Without it, Miller says, things could have gotten a lot worse. (This generous act may have also helped restore the young woman's faith in the male gender, but that's another story.) Miller's enterprising mother went on to become a hairdresser, ultimately owning a beauty parlor, while saving and buying a home of her own.

This incident represented Miller's first brush with philanthropy and helped her understand that even small gifts can lift people up in their hour of need. This story from her past animates her passion for her work.

Recently, Miller successfully secured a six-figure sponsorship from Food Lion, a Salisbury, North Carolina-based supermarket chain to upgrade and expand Wake Tech's food pantry program. "I realized that almost 50 percent of Wake Tech's students are food insecure," she says. "And 10 to 25 percent are hungry, meaning they went without food in the past month. No one can focus on schoolwork with a growling stomach."

Because the young fundraiser can feel in her gut what it means to be "without" (power, food, you name it); because her story aligns with Wake Tech's institutional "why" of supporting underserved students; and because she can tell the story with feeling, Miller has been remarkably successful in her efforts.

"Roxanne is a rock star," says her boss, Matt Smith, Wake Tech's vice president of development & strategic partnerships. "Her approach is amazingly effective."

Indeed, it feeds her soul to identify resources—from scholarship aid, to gap funding for books, medical and other emergency bills—so that students can stay in school, graduate, and have the ability to improve their lot in life. Just as Miller and her mother have done.

GETTING TO YOUR "WHY"

In Simon Sinek's popular and groundbreaking book, *Start with Why: How Great Leaders Inspire Everyone to Take Action*, he makes the case that what separates the true giants from the wannabes is understanding and being able to articulate their "why," and then creating a great enterprise based on that. Sinek's framework for this formulation is his now-famous golden circle. You can visualize it as a bull's eye containing three concentric circles: *Why* at the center; *How* in the next ring; and *What* in the final ring.

The philosopher Friedrich Nietzsche prefigured Sinek's formulation when he wrote, "He who has a *why* to live can bear almost any *how*."

In the business world, "what" represents your products; "how" stands for your business differentiators—the things that make you different from the next guy or gal; but your "why" is your *raison d'être*, your company's core purpose or belief system. Sinek cites the ultimate disruptor company Apple to illustrate his point. Apple's "why" was not to sell product, but to "Think different," to think outside the box.

"He who has a *why* to live can bear almost any *how.*" —Friedrich Nietzsche

Our work with advancement programs tells us that like Roxanne Miller, every development officer should be able to connect their personal "why" to their institutional "why." If they can't find or forge a meaningful connection, they may not be a good fit for this work.

When we onboard a new client, in the majority of cases, we begin with an assessment of the entire staff utilizing Wiley's ProfileXT Development Star assessment. Clients are provided the standard assessment, which pinpoints where they stand along a spectrum from low to high on such key metrics as verbal skill, assertiveness, sociability, manageability, and decisiveness. We then compare individual results to the proprietary results of the Advisory Board Gifted and Talented Study, which identifies and aggregates the characteristics of top-performing development professionals.

Spoiler alert: the data demonstrates that superstar fundraisers share similar characteristics. They are *creative* and *entrepreneurial,* and *prioritize people service.* What's more, these star performers are deeply connected to the mission of their nonprofit.

> The data demonstrates that superstar
> fundraisers share similar characteristics.
> They are creative and entrepreneurial, and
> prioritize people service. What's more,
> these star performers are deeply connected
> to the mission of their nonprofit.

A wholesale absence of these qualities in staffers does not bode well for your development team. I once interviewed every member of the sizable development staff of a client, a major university, asking all of the directors of development and major gift officers why they came to work. The overwhelming majority told me things like, "I have two kids to put through college." "It pays the mortgage, and the benefits are good." Only a few of this group said, "To help the students receive an education." Like Miller, these outliers were genuinely committed and connected to their work and as such set themselves up for top performance. Kudos to them.

However, more concerning to me was the rest of the group. Their answers revealed an endemic lack of engagement, suggesting trouble ahead both for the individuals (by not living their purpose) and for the institution in its long-term effectiveness. In short, it fell to me to share this insight with my client: "You will be far better served when your employees are aligned with your mission." The first step toward making change: I recommended that students be invited to attend meetings and engage with development staff. In addition, development officers took the ProfileXT assessment, which helped them zero in on their purpose and find ways to enhance the qualities that would help them be better fundraisers. To that end, we challenge all our clients to identify their "why."

Doing this exploratory self-assessment work and combining it with personal stories and messaging can help build interpersonal insights that enable caring connection and collaborative support teamwide. Like joy, reaching deep within for story and a sense of purpose can quite literally bring team members back to life—or *to* life for the very first time.

SELF-ASSESSMENTS: FIND YOUR "WHY" AND KNOW YOUR STRENGTHS

To help find your "why," according to research by Know Your Why™, all of us fall under one of nine categories. Which category best captures you?

1. To Contribute to a Greater Cause, Make a Difference, Add Value, or Have an Impact

2. To Create Relationships Based on Trust

3. To Make Sense Out of Things

4. To Find a Better Way and Share it

5. To Do Things the Right Way

6. To Think Different and Challenge the Status Quo

7. To Seek Mastery

8. To Create Clarity

9. To Simplify

To help you assess your greatest strengths, which often reinforce your "why," ask yourself the following key questions:

1. What brings you to life?

2. Can you name your strengths?

3. What do you do better than almost anyone?

4. When you do volunteer work, what is it?

5. What is your legacy?

MAKING A "WHY" BOOK

To enhance this building of culture and connection internally, at BrightDot we have created a team "why" book, which features a page for each team member. It's like a bio but deeper and more evocative. We have this material laid out professionally to share internally and sometimes make it available to our clients and prospects so they can get to know us better. It includes:

- Headshot
- Contact information
- Birthday (without the year)
- Children and grandchildren
- Hobbies
- Alma mater
- One-sentence summation of the person's personal philosophy
- And, you guessed it—favorite childhood toy

TELLING YOUR STORY

Once staffers have gone through the assessment phase and determined their "why," we recommend that they turn their attention to developing their personal stories. Ideally a coach, consultant, or supervisor would be tasked with working with them individually on this exercise.

Remember that this deep work demands vulnerability, courage, and truthfulness, so proceed with sensitivity. Start by challenging individuals to draw deep within themselves to find stories that are meaningful. Then, ask them to make connections between these stories and the institutional mission.

After the individual stories are developed, we recommend sharing them in a group setting. If your staff meets regularly for retreats, consider devoting time to this exercise.

> "A clear sense of purpose enables you to focus your efforts on what matters most, compelling you to take risks and push forward regardless of the odds or obstacles."
> —Margie Warrell
> Author of *Stop Playing Safe: Rethink Risk. Unlock the Power of Courage. Achieve Outstanding Success.*

The Miracle League story

I wasn't the least bit surprised when Michael Strader, a clutch member of the BrightDot team, selected the Miracle League of the Triangle, one of our early clients, for his first storybook contribution. In one fell swoop, his narrative combines the power of joy and identifying the right messaging. His story goes like this:

> "The Miracle League offers the baseball experience for those impacted by physical and mental challenges. When BrightDot first engaged with this nonprofit, their messaging was all about baseball. Bill and I spent months working with their staff and board to achieve

higher efficiencies and improve fundraising results. As a part of the process, we began attending Miracle League games, watching the action on the field. The smile on the face of a child in a wheelchair being wheeled around the baseball diamond, as if she had hit a home run, conveyed an exuberance you rarely experience in life. You could see her face light up when she reached home base. What was happening in the stands was almost as remarkable. There, we saw pure joy on the faces of siblings, parents, and grandparents who most of the time had to struggle to care for their loved ones."

After witnessing this powerful experience more than once, Michael and I advised Miracle League board members and staff to shift their messaging from focusing on baseball to focusing joy. Their eyes widened and their mouths fell open as they realized our advice was on target. It was not about *how* they did what they did, it was all about their *why*. Messaging about baseball was the factual approach. Messaging about joy tugged at heartstrings. Once the Miracle League fully embraced and incorporated this shift in messaging, their fundraising numbers grew rapidly, an upward spiral that continues to this day.

The Holiday Card story project

Another anecdote that exemplifies the power of stories that touch hearts and inspire action was written by BrightDot team member Kim Turner. Just as Roxanne Miller's childhood adversity informs her philanthropic purpose, Turner retrieved a memorable, mid-career encounter that transformed her thinking about the profession and the power of giving. Here it is:

"I'll never forget the sound of those bells. It was late one evening, and I was finishing up after a long day as director of the Children's Cancer Center at Phoenix Children's Hospital. It was mid-December and our annual Holiday Card Project—which raised $350,000 a year—was in full swing.

My colleague Robert and I were running late on this particular day, so after we finished preparing a $10,000 cash deposit, I told him to head on out. I had a few more things to do and then would be doing the same. As he said goodbye and opened the door, I remember hearing the chime of the bells.

It wasn't long before I heard the door bells chime again. "I wonder what he forgot," I thought. Looking up, much to my surprise, instead of Robert I saw a dirty, disheveled man at the doorway. Obviously homeless, he wore a long overcoat partially covering torn, baggy clothes. Even more concerning was the confused, dazed look on his face.

As he walked toward me, my initial response was that of fear, and my mind raced as I tried to figure out what to do. What happened next has been blazoned in my mind ever since. As he stopped right in front of me—about an arm's length away—he slowly lifted his hand to reveal a dime perched between his thumb and forefinger. He held it up proudly in front of my face.

"I want to help kids with cancer."

How unexpected. Instead of giving out of abundance, like many of us do, this dear man's gift was truly sacrificial and could only have come from a loving heart. As I look back on that moment, I often think about what would have happened if I would have welcomed him with a genuine smile and kind words.

That one interaction has taught me lasting lessons about human dignity and respect, grace and humility, and about how making false assumptions robs us of authentic and meaningful connections with others. I also learned about the power of giving, which is not just reserved for the wealthy and comfortable. Everyone has the right to experience the joy of helping those in need. Even those in need.

As a nonprofit professional who works with people from all walks of life, I realize how blessed I am to have the opportunity to help others experience the joy of giving, no matter who they are and no matter the size of their gift. There is no greater joy than that."

> The power of giving is not just reserved for the wealthy and comfortable. Everyone has the right to experience the joy of helping those in need. Even those in need.

MAKING AN INTERNAL STORYBOOK

"If I look at the mass, I will never act. If I look at the one, I will." —Mother Teresa

Similar to our BrightDot "why" book, we have created an in-house storybook. It is essentially a collection of transformative and touching client stories. Everyone on our team is challenged to contribute stories that have moved them and were transformational in their development. The book lives on our hard drive and is also contained in an old-fashioned three-ring binder so it can be expanded. And, remember, it's never finished. The stories not only paint a picture of what we do but they also become messages that anyone on the team can use to talk about our work and the impact we've had—individually and collectively.

GUIDING PRINCIPLES

The creation of your team's guiding principles is another important exercise to consider as part of your cultural work. This can be performed at a staff retreat or meeting. Distinct from the organization's mission statement, your guiding principles represent your team's core values, principles, or shared beliefs. President Jimmy Carter's powerful statement, "We must adjust to changing times and still hold to unchanging principles," sums up the concept beautifully. What are the "unchanging principles" to which you and your organization adhere, as times, programs, and even personnel change?

> "We must adjust to changing times and still hold to unchanging principles."
> —President Jimmy Carter

ROTARY INTERNATIONAL'S FOUR-WAY TEST

One of the most famous examples of organizational guiding principles is Rotary International's "Four-Way Test." Since the Four-Way Test was introduced in 1932, it has been used at Rotary Clubs worldwide and translated into over 100 languages. In many clubs, it is recited at every meeting. The test—which is offered in the form of questions about what "things we think, say and do"— stands as an ethical compass for the organization's beliefs and a reminder to club members of their core values. It is a simple set of principles that can steer any group of people in the right direction.

1. Is it the TRUTH?

2. Is it FAIR to all concerned?

3. Will it build GOODWILL and BETTER FRIENDSHIPS?

4. Will it be BENEFICIAL to all concerned?

To facilitate the creation of your own guiding principles, you will want to gather your team in a room and have a scribe take down ideas. Ask for key words and phrases that describe your team culture. For instance, during a recent client staff retreat, team members put up the following concepts: "kindness," "clarity," "transparency," and "willingness to fail." You can use pillar words or concepts. You may want to add an explanatory phrase to refine each key word.

Once you've settled on your principles, I recommend that you frame and post them in a common area of your office for all to see.

As an example, at BrightDot, our guiding principles take the form of five pillar words to which we adhere in all our work. They are:

- **Authentic**—Being who you are. Each team member's "why" informs the firm's "why" to impact lives.

- **Courageous**—Being honest with yourself and with others. We have found that too often in our clients' cultures, being kind takes the place of being honest. Holding someone accountable is hard because we might hurt someone's feelings. Courage is the ability to overcome fear and anxiety to take action.

- **Mindful**—We are under such pressure to perform at high levels that we are in "go mode" all the time. Mindfulness is being able to step back, take a deep breath, and look constructively at your work, your relationships, and your life. Even before NASCAR pit crews spring into 18 seconds of action, they pause ever so briefly to prepare mentally.

- **Resilient**—The ability to be tough and pick yourself up when things do not go your way. *Grit*, according to author Angela Ducksworth, is a combination of resilience, determination, and perseverance, which taken together "predict success."

- **Genius**—The ability to marry knowledge (insights learned) with wisdom (insights earned). Where these two intersect, genius can occur. High emotional intelligence is the result of this convergence.

Culture building with personal touchstones

To help with the continuous development of our culture at BrightDot, we believe informal storytelling is important, too, and can help us live our guiding principles. I think of these everyday stories and conversations as personal touchstones that build trust, connection, and caring. We schedule one-day meetups several times throughout the year to discuss business development and to work on culture. For our regular weekly or biweekly meetings, we always kick off our calls by asking a soft, nonbusiness question of each team member, such as "What is your favorite number and why?" "Favorite teacher?" "Your worst mistake?"

The questions are distributed a day or two in advance of the meeting so people have some time to reflect upon what they will say. The answers to these questions are generally brief, but they allow us to get to know each other better, building on that knowledge on a regular basis.

DEVELOPING DONOR-FACING MESSAGING

The work that you have just done in bringing your staff into alignment with their "why" as well as in having them develop a repertoire of personal and institutional stories— if executed properly—sets the stage for the next phase of developing compelling messages. That is, connecting with donors.

There are many elements to bringing heart to our engagements with possible funders, but we start with three key tools:

- an elevator speech—with a disarmingly simple and direct approach,

- an investor case statement—with the just-right level of detail,

- and a visual aid or metaphor, which we call "The Dead Skate."

The elevator speech

One of the most basic tools that every fundraiser should have at the tip of their tongue is an elevator speech. Doubtless you've heard of this term before. A young entrepreneur walks into an elevator with Warren Buffett and has 15 seconds to make their pitch. What do they say? If you don't have a high-level pitch already formulated, you may find yourself grasping for words.

The same elevator speech concept is needed for your nonprofit or university as you seek to attract more supporters. Please don't dismiss this "speech" idea as contrived and phony. Think of it rather as a communications tool to convey basic information about what you do, so you never find yourself going down a long, meandering path without getting to the point. The elevator speech is a starting point and conversation starter. If done well and delivered with sincerity, your discussion can go in any number of directions.

Your elevator speech needs to be open-ended and broad, but start off by touching the heart. Here's the basic formula we recommend; use the words below to start yourself off.

YOU KNOW HOW…
WHAT WE DO IS…
SO THAT.…

For Big Brothers Big Sisters of the Triangle, following is what was created at a recent retreat that we facilitated.

"YOU KNOW HOW in the Triangle the economy is thriving and yet the number of at-risk children who lack basic needs is growing?"

"WHAT WE DO IS provide positive mentor relationships that support at-risk children and their families."

"SO THAT through these relationships, our children develop confidence to change their worlds and ours!"

Again, your elevator speech can be crafted as a group exercise, but remember the KISS rule—*keep it simple, stupid*. I've seen too many nonprofits trip over themselves by trying to add too many details and nuance. When that happens, it's no longer an *elevator* speech. Keep it lean. Detail, nuance, and, yes, even story development come later.

BRIGHTDOT'S ELEVATOR SPEECH

Practicing what we preach and teach, we crafted our own elevator speech at one of our meetups. Here it is:

YOU KNOW HOW organizations are under tremendous pressure to raise money?

WHAT WE DO IS assemble a team of experts that brings a unique, holistic, heart-based approach to top performance.

SO THAT our clients raise more money and impact more lives.

Investor Case Statement

While in the past, institutional and nonprofit development officers devoted massive amounts of time to generating complex case statements full of data, statistics, and pie charts, we recommend going in another direction. The investor case statement piece that we have created is crafted expressly for the purpose of appealing to major donors.

Think about it: your best major gift prospects are people with more money than time. What they seek is high-level information—they do not want to get into the weeds of your work. What proves to be most impactful is messaging that touches their emotions. Remember, effective messaging is not about your organization; it's about the beneficiaries of your work and the transformation the donor can help facilitate.

> Remember, effective messaging is not about your organization; it's about the beneficiaries of your work and the transformation the donor can help facilitate.

The simplicity of this approach will doubtless require a mind shift for some advancement professionals. But remember, should a prospect or donor want more detail, you can always bring it to your next call, or you send it after your meeting in a follow-up or proposal.

Knowing that highly produced, glossy, four-color pieces are a turnoff to many donors who want their money going to mission rather than marketing, we recommend an investor case statement that is simple in construction and relatively inexpensive to produce. To that end, we provide clients with a black-and-white template featuring customizable components that can be inserted into the pockets of the folder.

> Highly produced, glossy, four-color pieces are a turnoff to many donors who want their money going to mission rather than marketing.

Customizable folder components

1. The folder. The cover folder presents a straightforward emotional appeal in bold lettering on the front. We do not include the nonprofit's or college's name or logo here. (You can include a modest-size version of your logo on the folder's back cover.)

For example, when working with the United Way of Coastal Fairfield County in Connecticut, which was in launch mode for its collective impact work for underserved babies, our cover message was: IT'S ALL ABOUT THE BABIES. Similarly, you'll need to work to refine and present a basic concept that reaches the heart.

Inside the folder, we recommend including the following key pages. All of them will carry a bold headline at the top, and the typeface will be large and readable, at least 14 point. With this messaging, brevity is paramount.

2. Overview sheet. For the overview sheet, which comes at the front of the case statement, we recommend the following template which communicates urgency.

The Time Is Now
WHY:

HOW:

WHAT:

After each of these colons, you'll need to include concise and moving messaging, no more than a line or two.

3. Situation. This sheet provides key bullet points about the problem your nonprofit or educational institution is facing. I tell clients, we're all fighting an "enemy," and here's the chance to name it/them. If you're Susan G. Komen, your enemy is breast cancer.

If you represent a homeless shelter, on this sheet you will provide the numbers of people in your area without a home. Include other key, relevant data points, such as the number of homeless people suffering from mental health issues, the number of school children who are unhoused, the difficulties of securing gainful employment when homeless, etc.

4. Impact. Here you present the solution your organization provides with data and other outcomes.

You may include such information as how many families you have helped to place in housing; the financial impact of becoming housed in terms of securing jobs; or a quote from a local newspaper saluting the transformative nature of your work.

5. *Solution.* The top of this sheet offers a bold headline, such as "The Cornerstone Village Opportunity," followed by the dollar goal, and additional high-level bullet points, outlining the vision and the opportunity for an investor to solve the problem.

6. *Impactful Initiatives.* Assuming you have multiple initiatives to fund or varying offers, this sheet provides your menu of needs with price tags included.

7. *Your Opportunity.* The last sheet in the folder is customizable to the person/entity to whom you are making your ask. At the top of the sheet, in bold, is "Your Opportunity." Next comes a generic invitation to impact lives through the organization. Below that is space to make your specific appeal to your donor. You should invite the prospect to invest in a specific project, or piece of a project, and include a dollar amount.

THE DEAD SKATE: THANKING YOUR DONOR

In addition to taking a new approach to investor case statements, I always ask clients to review their donor acknowledgment messaging. Sadly, in far too many development offices, donor acknowledgment messaging is almost an afterthought. If you have the gift in hand, the rationale goes, why waste time on the thank you letter? Indeed, the same tired acknowledgment letters are often used year in and year out, without even being revisited or refreshed.

The truth is that thanking donors is just as critical for connecting with donors as is authentic, on-target messaging. Probably more so. Research shows that less than 25 percent of all first-time donors ever make a second gift. When asked the reason, many say they didn't give again because they were not thanked appropriately for their first gift. We have come to understand that getting to the heart of a donor can pull in the first gift but if you want the second, you must once again reach their heart in expressing appreciation and emphasizing impact.

> Research has shown that less than 25 percent of all first-time donors ever make a second gift. When asked the reason, many say they didn't give again because they were not thanked appropriately for their first gift.

The term "dead skate" carries a very special meaning for my firm as it is a tool that we developed back in 2014 for our very first client, The Hope Center for Kids in Omaha,

Nebraska. The Hope Center—a remarkable nonprofit that started in 1998 as a skating rink for at-risk children in North Omaha—hired us to help build its major gift program.

When I made my first visit, while watching all the happy, energetic, elementary-age kids whirling around the rink— at least for a moment far from the scourge of gang violence plaguing their neighborhoods—I turned to Brenda Block, director of development, and asked, "Where do you keep all your dead skates?"

She shot me a blank look, puzzled at the term.

My youngest daughter was an aspiring ballerina, and I found myself buying countless pairs of pricey toe shoes. When a toe shoe breaks after a few months of active use, it becomes a "dead toe shoe." I explained this to Brenda, then asked where all the broken skates—the dead skates—were kept. She gestured to an overflowing closet then went over and retrieved one.

"Can you find a Sharpie?" I asked.

When she returned, I walked out on the rink and stopped a young skater named Jeremiah. I got on my knees to look him straight in the eye and asked him why he was there. He told me that his mother made him go "so I won't be shot and killed like my brother."

I asked him if he'd be willing to sign his name on the broken skate. Lit up with pride, he signed his name on the skate, then took off to skate.

Brenda and I came up with a plan—to take Jeremiah's "dead skate" to one of their previous donors. We also developed a script. She would ask for an appointment to stop by and say thank you. She'd present the signed skate, telling them that around 500 children had used a skate like this one during the past 10 years "because of your generosity." Then, I suggested she pause for a moment, before turning the skate around to reveal the autograph. At that point, she would tell the story of Jeremiah and why he came to the Hope Center.

Once Brenda got comfortable with the idea (and, yes, we rehearsed a few times), she found our experiment to be a resounding success. We learned that when donors were given dead skates and responded positively, they in turn became messengers for the Hope Center. If they displayed their skates on their desks at work or in their homes, every visitor who saw them would ask the significance. When this happened, donors' contributions became as regular as clockwork.

We've been using some variation of the dead skate for the majority of our clients ever since.

Let me leave you with a few concepts about dead skate messaging, so that you can develop your own version.

1. Every organization has a "dead skate"—you just have to find it.

2. When you identify your own winning dead skate, you'll know it because donors will respond positively and display them proudly, unlike plaques or computer-generated thank you letters. (You'll still need to send the thank you letters, which also stand as records for their tax returns.)

3. The messaging has to be about the person who benefits from the nonprofit, so be sure to include that beneficiary in some way in your dead skate (hence Jeremiah's signature).

MESSAGES WITH HEART ARE THE MESSAGES THAT MATTER

The work of messaging is like housework; it's never done. Programs change, evolve, and go away; donors emerge, engage, and ultimately move on. Vocabulary and even grammar change and evolve, and the top-notch advancement offices need to keep abreast of current times. I urge clients to never stint on investing in messaging.

As you review our tools, the common thread is that these messaging tools are not about you—the nonprofit—but about *them*, the donor, the prospect, and the people served.

As we've shown, compelling messages are important in three contexts: individually, inside your team, and outward facing. Story becomes a vehicle for personal growth and development. Once you take storytelling and message development seriously in the context of fundraising, you'll discover how it can transform your team and benefit your institution.

A BRIGHTDOT QUESTION:
"Storybooks for boards and other stakeholders"

We've demonstrated the value of creating stories for your staff, as individuals, and teamwide. The storybook tool is just as powerful for other stakeholders and supporters of your organization. Boards of directors, advisory committees, and alumni groups including reunion committees can use the methods presented here to create their own stories.

All you need to do is ASK THE QUESTIONS:

- What story connects you to our organization and mission?
- What is your "why" for joining in our work?

For instance, with a board of directors, you can set aside five minutes at each meeting for story sharing. Invite your staff members to share a story—either a personal one, connecting their "why" with the organizational mission, or a story about a volunteer or a client impacted by your team's work. This will connect board members to the development team and to the mission, while amassing a powerful advancement tool.

For instance, at the Chatham County Council on Aging, a nonprofit we have served, the story of Christine, a 92-year-old Meals on Wheels volunteer, continues to inspire all stakeholders. Christine serves as an unofficial "poster girl" for the Council because of this tireless nonagenarian's service to constituents—who are often a generation her junior. When the stories or examples are good, board members will remember them, repeat them, and be on the lookout for fresh examples. These stories serve to convert your supporters to raving advocates and stellar ambassadors for "the cause!"

PRINCIPLE #3

TAP THE POWER OF EMOTIONAL INTELLIGENCE

Emotions can get in the way
or get you on the way.
—*Mavis Mazhura*

Throughout the book, I've emphasized the primacy of tapping the emotional, human side of fundraising in driving success in your development office. In Principle #1, I unpacked how the "joy initiative" factored in the success of Meredith College's recent comprehensive campaign while providing ways to adopt similar measures in your own shop.

In Principle #2, we made the case that messaging—storytelling coming from a place of authentic feeling and a deep sense of why—is a force of nature you will want in your court. With it, we offer proven, hands-on tools for the creation of powerful messages that can light a fire under your staff, and then radiate outward to your organization, community and, ultimately, philanthropic partners.

Now, we're going to turn to the underpinnings of everything you've learned so far: The ever-evolving field of emotional intelligence. Here I will demonstrate how it can work for you as you tap into this rich fabric of human-connection capital.

Don't discount emotional intelligence as the "soft stuff." It is real, revealing, and a tool that can be harnessed. The intentional development and use of emotional intelligence are underutilized in the advancement field yet ideally suited to the work we do.

How you can harness the power of emotional intelligence to transform your educational or nonprofit development staff is the meat of this chapter. But before we delve into that, let's review the concept of emotional intelligence.

> The intentional development and use of emotional intelligence are underutilized in the advancement field yet ideally suited to the work we do.

EMOTIONAL INTELLIGENCE: A DIFFERENT WAY OF BEING SMART

The Cambridge Dictionary defines "emotional intelligence" as "the ability to understand the way people feel and react and to use this skill to make good judgments and to avoid or solve problems." The concept burst on the scene some 25 years ago upon the publication of Daniel Goleman's groundbreaking book *Emotional Intelligence: Why It Can Matter More Than IQ* (1995).

The five primary elements of emotional intelligence (EI) are:

1. **Self-awareness**—being in tune with your own feelings and understanding how they impact those around you.

2. **Self-regulation**—maintaining control of yourself. When perturbed, you "check yourself" so your emotions don't overpower your judgment; you rarely, if ever, act rashly or lash out at others.

3. **Motivation**—holding high personal standards and maintaining your drive in the face of setbacks, which is intrinsic to emotionally intelligent individuals.

4. **Empathy**—having the capacity to put yourself in another's shoes is the cornerstone of a person endowed with EI. You easily pick up on the states of mind of others by reading their body language, voiceprints, and other cues and clues.

5. **Social skills**—being able to communicate good or bad news and to rally others to your cause. The word "diplomatic" describes someone equipped with these social skills.

Each of these qualities connects to the other and amounts to what Goleman calls "a different way of being smart." Outside of academic settings, where students are judged on their ability to display their brilliance in test-taking, writing papers, and developing new ideas, being adept at this different way of being smart matters much more than stratospheric IQ numbers or a record of straight As.

Quite simply, academic proficiency and technical know-how are givens to gain entry into a professional field; however, star performers distinguish themselves by demonstrating such personal qualities as initiative and empathy, adaptability and persuasiveness, Goleman writes in *Working with Emotional Intelligence* (1998). His conclusions have received widespread confirmation in several cornerstone reports in the burgeoning academic field of philanthropic studies.

> Quite simply, academic proficiency and technical know-how are givens to gain entry into a professional field; however, star performers distinguish themselves by demonstrating such personal qualities as initiative and empathy, adaptability, and persuasiveness.

"CURIOUS CHAMELEONS"

Research confirms that EI is of paramount importance in the fundraising space. In the Education Advisory Board's (EAB) landmark 2015 study, *Gifted and Talented: What Makes a Top Fundraiser in the Age of Venture Philanthropy?*, results showed that 78 percent of top-performing fundraisers could be best described as "curious chameleons." Curious chameleons are individuals who exhibit intellectual and social curiosity; and flexibility in language and behavior; they enjoy gathering, processing, and synthesizing information; and are strategic solicitors who are unafraid to make the ask. These curious chameleons are closely aligned to the ENTJ personality type in the Myers-Briggs assessment (extroverted, intuitive, thinking, and judging). "This is the second-rarest personality type," according to the report, "and indicates that someone is achievement-oriented, confident, assertive and motivated." While ENTJs account for about 4 percent of the general population, they represent between 60 and 70 percent of top achievers in the field of advancement, the study shows.

> 78 percent of top-performing fundraisers could be best described as "curious chameleons."

The EAB study—which analyzed the contributions secured by 1,217 Major Gift Officers at 90 higher educational institutions in America and Great Britain—shows that these top performers represented just 3.8 percent of all the MGOs studied. Members of this elite group combined the best traits of each of the five distinct advancement profile types presented: the Cultivator, the Fixer, the Adapter, the Academic, and the Lone Ranger.

Likewise, the Human Capital Institute's 2013 report of star-performing advancement professionals, "Leadership and Emotional Intelligence: The Keys to Driving ROI and Organizational Performance," concluded that "what builds great and sustainable organizations are leaders with a high degree of business acumen, specific skills… and emotional intelligence."

Despite such well-regarded and high-level studies demonstrating the need for emotional intelligence in the fundraising field, our experience with clients shows that EI readiness and proficiency are not yet given their due in the hiring, training, and retention of fundraising professionals.

It is our desire for you—and for the field—that this will change dramatically in the coming years.

> "What builds great and sustainable organizations are leaders with a high degree of business acumen, specific skills... and emotional intelligence." —Human Capital Institute

A TRANSFORMATIVE GIFT: WHAT DOES A STAR PERFORMER LOOK LIKE?

I want to share a story about a development professional performing at the top of his game. He has been in the field of university advancement for over 20 years and has experienced his share of hills and valleys. Yes, he happens to be one of my coaching clients, but what's important here is how he tapped his emotional intelligence to bring in a transformative gift. It is a case study in what can happen when you're doing everything right, and firing on all cylinders. While not every development professional will be able to reel in a fish of this size, we can all learn how to be better fundraisers from North Carolina State University's Michael Ward.

"Relationship builder-in-chief"

It all started with a $1,000 gift. What drew notice at the development office of North Carolina State University (NC State) was the age of the donor. The check was written in November 2016 by Rede Wilson, a freshly minted graduate from the College of Textiles. How this gift became the gateway to a $28 million philanthropic investment from the Wilson family—in less than two years' time—has become the stuff of legend, not only on campus but also in development circles nationally.

"The first I heard about the gift was when I got a call from Joey Wilkerson, my colleague in Central Advancement," says Michael Ward, executive director at the North Carolina Textile Foundation and the person who is widely credited with orchestrating the transformative gift.

A first meeting in November 2017 in which Wilson and Ward connected with each other instantly—and jousted to outdo the other in the listening department—led to more face time and a deeper bond. Getting Rede's "Aunt Cres"— Elizabeth Wilson Calabrese, a 1989 College of Textiles graduate—on board, eventually led to an introduction to—and ultimately full-blooded commitment from— the family patriarch, Frederick "Fred" Eugene Wilson, Jr. Class of 1961. The headline-making gift, announced on November 2, 2018, was the largest ever made to the 120-year-old College of Textiles and represented only the second time that a college at NC State was named for a benefactor.

With any major fundraising victory, a number of factors come into play: a qualified and willing donor; an initiative that connects in deep ways with the donor's "why"; the right chemistry between the development personnel, institutional leadership, and the donor; and, finally, good timing. Michael Ward's sensitive, emotionally tuned approach to the process and to his prospective donors made all the difference.

Look for openings

Fred Wilson, the enormously successful CEO of the High Point, NC-based Piedmont Chemical Industries, Inc., a family-owned business offering chemical manufacturing services for the textile industry domestically and overseas, had been on NC State's radar for some time. Advancement officers knew that Wilson had a charitable heart, having made a multimillion-dollar commitment to High Point University back in 2011. However, repeated attempts to reach him had fallen short.

The arrival of Fred Wilson's grandson's gift provided a new opening. As the relationship developed with Rede Wilson, it was clear that the young man had "an enormous love" for the College of Textiles. Rede Wilson readily agreed to join the Dean's Young Alumni Leadership Council. "But probably the most auspicious clue early on," says Ward, "was his expressed desire for his family to get 'more involved.'"

Courtside courtship

Michael Ward understood that he needed to get better acquainted with Rede Wilson and the entire family. The development officer's heart soared when a devoted board member offered up four coveted courtside seats to the January 2018 NC State-Clemson game where Ward was able to host Rede Wilson along with David Hinks, Wilson's former college advisor, now dean of the College of Textiles. Providentially, the game turned out to be riveting, a real nail-biter. "It was an amazing opportunity for bonding," Ward recalls. "We were so close to the action you had to watch out for tripping refs. Talk about exciting—State won by one point!"

On that magical evening, Rede Wilson was asked how the team could get in front of Wilson's Aunt Cres. The following month, Ward found himself in the Chancellor's box for the NC State-Carolina game, along with Rede Wilson, Cres Calabrese, her husband, Mike, and son, Will Davis. Ward will never forget the date—February 10—which serendipitously turned out to be Rede Wilson's 25th birthday.

Several more meetings followed over the next several months, including an in-depth campus tour for the Calabreses of the College; lunch with students; and a visit with Calabrese's former advisor, Gary Mock. At that meeting, Mock presented Cres Calabrese with an autographed copy of his book, *A Century of Progress: The Textile Program, North Carolina State University: 1899–1999.* "Cres's emotional reaction told me how deeply she felt about the College and Gary Mock," he said.

Not long after, Ward asked Calabrese if she would commit to getting her father on campus in the summer. She agreed, but cautioned him not to pull any students out of class or roll out any red carpet. Buy him a hot dog for lunch, she joked.

Listen closely

Ward is nothing if not a good listener. "I've always believed that people tell you what they really want," he says, "and your gift to them is listening." Ward took Calabrese's insights about her father's down-home tastes to heart. Never let your assumptions about what a high net-worth individual would want, he says, override what people tell you.

> "I've always believed that people tell you what they really want and your gift to them is listening." —Michael Ward

When Fred Wilson came to campus in July 2018, Ward was able to make an impromptu hallway introduction to Chancellor Randy Woodson.

Fred Wilson was dressed in casual slacks, layered with a dusting of Carolina dirt.

"I apologize for looking so dapper," the chancellor quipped. "I dressed for a Kiwanis lunch."

Wilson retorted, "I put on my cleanest, dirtiest clothes for you!"

After more lighthearted banter with the chancellor, Wilson, and Vice Chancellor Brian Sischo, the Wilson family was taken for a casual lunch at the Lonnie Poole Clubhouse.

Establish trust: Be authentic

Michael Ward felt immediate chemistry with Rede Wilson, Cres Calabrese, and when he finally met Fred Wilson, with the textile magnate himself. "We have the same down-home values," says Ward. "He just has a larger pocketbook."

What's essential when dealing with donors, Ward says, is to establish a personal connection, to be authentic to who you are. Being yourself, in turn, allows donors to be who they are. It's essential, he advises, that you get this part right, before even thinking about "the ask."

Pace the ask

Once you've established that all-important connection to your donor, the development professional needs to "trust the process and let the speed of the process be dictated by the donors," he says.

In the case of the Wilsons, once it was clear that three generations of family members were on board and passionate about building the college's position as the global leader in textile education and innovation, there was no compelling reason to wait to present a proposal.

In consultation with Vice Chancellor Sischo and the team, Ward says, the ask was discussed at length. After some internal back and forth, in the end, Sischo deferred to Ward who was, after all, closest to the donors. "We settled on a meaningful number that we thought aligned with the values and the impact the family wanted to make," Ward recalls. "I cannot tell you how humbled I was when the vice chancellor trusted me to make the call on the amount and then move the gift forward."

Whatever the magic formula, Ward and the team at NC State hit just the right note. In a gathering of College of Textiles constituents, not long after the gift was announced, Cres Calabrese, who has since joined the board of the Wilson College of Textiles, called Ward "the relationship builder-in-chief, (my) newly adopted brother. His approach of a handshake and a hot dog won our hearts!"

Once you've established that all-important connection to your donor, the development professional needs to "trust the process and let the speed of the process be dictated by the donors." he says.

UNPACKING TOP PERFORMANCE: IT IS TEACHABLE

Michael Ward displays a myriad of skills that place him at the top of the charts in the emotional intelligence department. He's a good listener and team player—always quick to credit others whether they are subordinates, peers, or superiors, and always relating to others on a personal level. His down-home demeanor and humility are genuine, and Ward, an Eagle Scout, never wants to put anyone out. When he and I worked together, I couldn't help but notice his attention to detail, remarking on and remembering details that might escape others. A member of my team once asked Ward why his iPhone contact directory didn't include headshots. She then proceeded to add her photo into his contacts, showing him step by step how to do it. He never forgot this small gesture and thanks her every time they meet. While Ward's strong service orientation to others is a given, our coaching work together focused on his doing a better job of advocating for himself. (Ironically, many curious chameleons like Ward are so attuned to others that they can lose sight of themselves and their own needs.)

In this, he proved to be a quick study. In fact, his most recent accomplishment was his appointment as executive director of the North Carolina Textile Foundation.

Attaining "emotional attunement"

So how exactly does Michael Ward manage to forge a deep connection with prospects and donors that others find so difficult, if not impossible, to make? Of course, part of his ability is innate. He has a generous spirit, is other-oriented, and seeks to engage with and help everyone he meets. This positive energy fuels a feedback loop in which others are drawn to him.

This chemistry that Ward manages to so quickly establish is rooted in neuroscience. Citing a scholar's work examining the physiological interaction of married couples, Daniel Goleman shows how when two people come into true alignment, a form of mimicry occurs. This connected state is "a biological phenomenon called entrainment, a sort of intimate emotional tango," he writes in *Working with Emotional Intelligence*. This kind of rapport "demands we put aside our own emotional agendas for the time being so that we can clearly receive the other person's signals. When we are caught up in our own strong emotions, we are off on a different physiological vector, impervious to the more subtle cues that allow rapport."

When two people begin a conversation, if they are aligned, they fall into a rhythm of movements and gestures, even pauses. Facial expression is one of the most obvious outward expressions of any personal connection or interaction. "To the degree we take on the pace, posture, and facial expression of another person, we start to inhabit their emotional space," he writes, "as our body mimics the other's we begin to experience emotional attunement."

While it's clear that emotional attunement may come more naturally to some than others, the good news is that key components of emotional intelligence can be learned. Unlike IQ that is thought to be fixed by early adulthood, your emotional intelligence can continue to develop with age, especially when you challenge yourself to improve. Just as identifying powerful stories that connect your "why" to your organization's "why" is mission-critical for improving what you say, sharpening your "soft skill set" is a way to develop your EI repertoire so that you open your aperture to tune into others.

> Unlike IQ that is thought to be fixed by early adulthood, your emotional intelligence can continue to develop with age, especially when you challenge yourself to improve.

DEVELOPING YOUR EI REPERTOIRE

Let's return to the five characteristics of an emotionally intelligent person and share specific steps to develop your

EI quotient. Following are some concepts we share with clients that will work for you as well.

1. *Self-awareness:* The ability to own your emotions and understand how they impact you is the first step to deepening your innate emotional intelligence. To develop self-awareness, we suggest keeping a journal. Even investing just five minutes a day reviewing and recording your thoughts and actions, your high moment of the day (and your low) can help usher in enhanced self-awareness. If you only have time for a minute a day, try a gratitude journal where you write down the one thing for which you were most grateful. It can be as inane as, "Being first in line at Starbucks because after I placed my order, a long line formed" or as profound as "The offer on our new home was accepted!"

Debriefing exercise: A lesson I took away from interviewing a group of top gun pilots is to debrief immediately after every significant meeting or call. Borrowing from them, we recommend a debrief. Ask yourself, how could *I* have done better? Expressed myself better? With a donor, did I present a follow-up item that would make a return visit the natural next step? (Please note that the focus is always on you and your performance, not on how Gerry or Karla behaved at the meeting.)

2. *Self-regulation:* Improving your ability to self-regulate will require an honest review of how you respond to failure or difficult situations. When something goes wrong, is your automatic response to blame someone else, or do you always look to your part—no matter how minimal—in the matter? If you're a blamer, you will need to take stock and start holding yourself accountable. If you own up to your part of any setback, your coworkers will be appreciative and likely follow suit.

Self-regulation also applies to how your treat yourself. Are you too hard on yourself? Do you have a glass jaw, meaning that one hard punch will knock you out? If so, you need to develop the ability to deconstruct the blow while placing it in the context of the larger picture. And remember, once you've examined the situation carefully, you need to ease up and let it go.

3. *Motivation:* How do you develop—or deepen—your motivation? As discussed in Principle #2, it starts with identifying your "why." Why do you do the work you do? If, quite frankly, you're just in it for the paycheck, you either need to start looking for a new job or focus on forging a deeper connection with your work. Setting goals for yourself—where do you want to be in six months, three years, five years, and where do you want your institution to be—is enormously useful as a starting point.

4. Optimism: Top performers tend to be optimistic and are able to shake off disappointment while reframing their reaction to any situation. Finding the one silver lining after an accident or disappointment characterizes motivated individuals. It is a healthy adaptive change that you can make. Yes, you had a fender bender, but at least now you will get your car painted—something you'd been putting off for months. Or, sorry that your new development director resigned but with the salary savings, you'll now be able to greenlight the staff retreat your team has been clamoring for, etc…. You get the idea. Train yourself to see sunny skies ahead—always.

5. Empathy: How do you develop the empathy muscle or reflex? Everyone knows you need to listen more than talk, but it's not just giving the other person the microphone, it's the *quality* of your listening that counts. True empathy lies in connecting to the other person's emotions and caring about them as an individual, in a context outside of your immediate objective. When listening, be fully present with what the other person is saying, rather than focusing on your thoughts or rehearsing what you plan to say next. Pay attention to their body language and tone so *you can respond to the speaker's feelings* rather than the literal script. I remember once going into a pitch meeting that I expected would go well. Inside, one of the three interviewers had a scowl on her face and arms clamped across her chest. Even though I tried to break through during the hourlong session, I realize now that her body language told me everything I needed to know.

6. *Social skills:* Social skills endow you with grace and, when developed, provide a behavioral roadmap to most every situation, including moments of turbulence and surprise. As with developing motivation, one of the best tools I recommend is the *reframing method.* A wise person once said that nothing is ever as good—or as bad—as it initially appears. Remind yourself that this too will pass. At the office, take on the role of mediator, the person who sees both sides of any situation and can add a moment of levity or perspective to a conflict or disappointment. If the cookies are burnt for the office party, say, "Hey, well at least we won't be tempted to break our diets tonight!" And don't forget to use *the powerful tool of praise* with others. Most people crave positive feedback, and few of us get enough of it. Praise opens doors and advances friendship. Giving a compliment is just as important as receiving one. And there's more: because it puts you (the giver) in a positive frame of mind—just seeing the beaming response on the recipient's face—it can just make your day!

SOME LESSONS ON EMOTIONAL INTELLIGENCE IN THE DEVELOPMENT FIELD

I'd like to devote the remainder of this chapter to several specific concepts that relate to emotional intelligence that I have observed throughout my collegiate career as well as when working with nonprofit and higher ed clients. You can apply important lessons to your own realm from these insights and ideas.

1. Though Meredith College's comprehensive campaign (please see Principle #1) was already underway when we were hired, the campaign had reached its inevitable mid-course doldrums. Vice President for Advancement Lennie Barton heard me speak at a conference about the correlation between emotionally intelligent fundraisers and enhanced performance and decided to provide our ProfileXT Development Star assessment to his entire advancement team. Once results were in, he hired us to provide EI coaching for five MGOs whom we believed would benefit the most. In the truth-is-stranger-than-fiction category, Barton recalls, "the coaching work revealed that one MGO in particular had a distaste for making phone calls." Once that issue surfaced and our coach worked with the woman to build her confidence and establish accountability tools, he says, she became "one of our best producers to close out the campaign. As a result of the training, she realized a $5 million gift and two $1 million gifts helping to send the final numbers above goal."

2. **Pointers and red flags for new hires.** Other clients, such as the United Way of South Hampton Roads in Virginia, also had all development staff members take our assessment and asked us to deliver a team report to identify strengths and weaknesses of both individual members and the entire team, along with suggestions for improvement. Other clients, including a number of United Ways and colleges such as Guilford and Barton in North Carolina, are now using our assessment service to screen top job candidates *before* an offer is made. (See more in Principle #2.)

When you're interviewing candidates for a position, we suggest you pay close attention to nonverbal clues and consider how they perform when viewed through the human connectivity lens. Do they make good eye contact? Do they clasp your hand warmly? Do they strike you as happy? Do *they* ask questions about you and your organization?

What is more, watch out for the overuse of the perpendicular pronoun. Meredith College President Jo Allen cautions anyone interviewing a prospective development director to look out for one of the biggest and brightest of red flags.

"If someone says, '*I* brought in a $5 million gift,' or '*I* raised most of the funds for a recent campaign,' proceed with caution," she says. "In reality, it's almost never the case that an individual did something on her own or in a vacuum. Amazing results are almost always a result of team effort."

"If someone says, 'I brought in a $5 million gift,' or 'I raised most of the funds for a recent campaign,' proceed with caution. In reality, it's almost never the case that an individual did something on her own or in a vacuum. Amazing results are almost always a result of team effort."
—Dr. Jo Allen,
president Meredith College

"Ask for feedback and you'll get a gift; ask for a gift and you'll get feedback."

3. **I can think of almost no field in which one's listening skills matter more. I always advise all clients to improve their listening skills.** If you prefer talking to listening, or you are not a natural listener, the following observations and suggestions will help you develop your skills:

- Think of listening as *active engagement*. Listening well is never passive. Do not allow your mind to wander or drift when in conversation. Do not think about what you're making for dinner or wonder how your son did on his driver's exam. Focus on the speaker's words, and try to remember what they are saying.

- *Find a quiet space for conservation.* If you're at a restaurant or coffee shop and the music is too loud, ask to have the volume turned down. If it's an important meeting, check out the venue before you meet for noise level.

- *Maintain eye contact* throughout the conversation.

- *Repeat words* back to the person you're speaking with verbatim, or try to recap what has been said. For example, "So you're telling me that because your family moved so much, you never really felt you had a home." This will then encourage them to expand on the theme. It also demonstrates your interest in what is being said.

- *Put your phone away.* Never be found guilty of *phubbing* (or phone snubbing). We advise all our clients to put away their cell phones in meetings, inside or outside the office.

- *Don't try to steer the conversation* in any set course or interrupt by offering suggestions. Listen with your heart!

4. **Move outside your comfort zone.** We've found that once clients begin to get too comfortable with their work—too attached to their routine—they are not only leaving money on the table but leaving creative energy and the possibility of growth there, too. "Show up where you are expected *and* where you are not expected," is on the list of personal guiding principles created by Dr. Scott Ralls, president of Wake Technical Community College. At BrightDot, this concept carries great resonance and is well worth repeating.

5. **Develop a wide network and circle of acquaintances**. Whenever you meet star performers, you will invariably find that they have a wide circle of acquaintances. Witness Michael Ward who cultivates, cares about, and maintains relationships with subordinates, peers, and superiors. Remember the curious chameleon, who takes time to take it all in, who makes acquaintances and connections with a variety of people. Having a wide and varied circle serves to spark creativity, as you take ideas from one person or place, like a bumblebee, and deliver them to another. At a college or university, top fundraisers make themselves known in academic circles, keeping abreast of the latest research in numerous fields. They follow student trends on campus as well as community and world issues.

6. **"Everyone is a fundraiser."** Another characteristic of any development office worth emulating is that *everyone* on the organization's staff—accountants, executive assistants, members of the grounds crew—feels that they are a change agent and charged with raising money. A high-functioning team owns the mission and shows pride in its success. I'll never forget reading about a study of the culture at NASA back in the 1970s. The interview team at the Johnson Space Center spoke with virtually every employee there, asking them to share details of their job. During one session, a member of the janitorial crew exclaimed, "What do you mean, what do I *do*? I put a man on the moon!" This wise soul understood connectivity and had taken the NASA mission to heart.

7. **Flight teams at Georgetown College.** The creation of "flight teams" is a strategy for you to consider in order to break down silos inside your organization. All too often, employees from different departments don't know each other, so they miss the chance to be part of a team and to put their heads together to address common problems.

I came to this conclusion as president of Georgetown College when I realized that hidden within certain departments were talents that, if discovered, could have a huge impact on creating something wonderful. As a result, we created four "flight teams," each team made up of positive-thinking individuals representing every department on our campus, including marketing, admissions, development, and grounds. Each team was given a challenge to think about strategically and tasked with bringing back a solution. Once a month, all the flight teams met and shared their progress.

The goal of one of the teams was to improve the experience of first-time visitors to the campus. Everyone who participated contributed outstanding ideas. Then I stumbled on Tiffany Hornberger. She was associate director of financial aid whose job was to meet with students and help them create strategies to bolster their financial aid packages. What I found out by accident was that not too many years before, she had been a character at Disney World.

Who would know more about first impressions than an employee of the Magic Kingdom? What she shared with us was basic but fundamental: *the importance of simple things, like smiles, and cleanliness everywhere on campus.* At Disney properties, she explained, crews go to work every night making the place spotless. They not only do the obvious—like cleaning bathrooms and picking up litter—but they scrape gum from the sidewalks and spray them down to remove spilled soda, ketchup, and the like. Hornberger's input raised the insights of this first flight team to new heights!

Morale on campus improved as new friendships blossomed among individuals on the flight teams. Many had worked on the same campus for years but never spoken. The benefit to the college was new ideas and strategic thinking.

Employees found this initiative empowering. I will never forget the excitement when our chief of security, Dan Brown, stopped me on campus with a suggestion. "Why don't we create a campus-wide initiative for members of the security and grounds crew to check the tires on all the students' cars and wash all their windshields the day before the drive home for holidays and semester break?"

I immediately approved the idea. Because Brown felt empowered as a member of the flight team, he acted as a cultural change agent, adding a new benefit for students and their parents. This six-times-a-year ritual became our going-away protocol. The response from parents, grandparents, and even a few appreciative students was immediate and overwhelmingly positive.

8. **Accountability is a powerful tool.** Back in 2017, I was brought in by Barbara Mulkey to work on board development with the General Hugh Shelton Leadership Center at North Carolina State University. The Center's mission is to inspire, educate, and develop

values-based leaders who are committed to personal integrity, professional ethics, and selfless service.

I've always found that highly successful people thrive on accountability. They perform at their best when they make specific commitments and know that they will be reporting back. When I addressed the Shelton Center Board, I shared what top-performing boards typically do in terms of scorecards, monetary commitments, and the like. Luckily, General Shelton himself happened to be in the room.

After I made my presentation, he piped up, saying, "I only surround myself with top performers!"

As a result of his endorsement—without hesitation—the board voted to step up to a new level, including asking of themselves and each other to make cash-flow gifts each year as well as agree to donate an asset gift before stepping off the board. As a result of this board training, the Shelton Center for Leadership has pulled in more money, including the receipt of its largest gift to date!

9. **Finally, if an organization's leaders are not curious, open, and coachable, your lift will be much steeper.** We have been hired a number of times by organizations wanting us to improve the results of their development teams. The greatest lesson we have learned is that if the boss or supervisor is not

coachable—isn't willing to look in the mirror and change the culture from the top down—then the ability to introduce the tools of emotional intelligence to the staff becomes much more challenging. While some useful work can be done on an individual basis, in order to bring about transformative, system-level change, *everyone needs to be on board, especially leadership.*

A BRIGHTDOT QUESTION:
"Are you 100 percent present?"

Recently, I stumbled upon a key awareness tool that is powerful. Jan and I have a routine where when I return home after a day of meetings or from a trip, the two of us pour a glass of wine and go on our back porch and catch up. Our goal is to listen and affirm each other. Recently I dragged home exhausted from a three-day trip. Jan, on the other hand, was animated. She had a lot to share about a recent conversation with one of her homeless friends she saw that day at the meal ministry at our church. As she excitingly began to relay her story, I realized I was barely listening. I interrupted, "Jan, I am fascinated by the amazing work you and the other volunteers do, but I am so tired I am only listening at 25 percent. If you will wait until the morning, I will give you 100 percent of my attention." She waited.

The next day it struck me: Could this be the key to demonstrating top emotional intelligence?

It required honesty and courage on my part to tell her I wasn't fully there for her. It required social awareness on her part to accept my request to delay.

What if in every conversation with a supervisor, an employee, a donor, or intimate, you stopped and asked yourself, "Am I 100 percent present in this conversation?" If I am only 90 percent there, and my mind is flitting elsewhere, I'm cheating myself… and someone else, too.

Being 100 percent present demonstrates top emotional intelligence. My challenge to you is to check yourself in every conversation, and either rise to the 100 percent level, or be honest and vulnerable enough to share your current state of mind. If you're not fully present, you should reschedule your talk. Practice it…it builds trusting relationships.

AFTERWORD

I have been wanting to write *Start with Heart* since I began work in development almost 40 years ago. I am a firm believer in the multiplier effect, that is, when you impact one life, you're really impacting 15, and those 15 will impact another 15, and before long, you will have touched millions of lives.

But what I know now and didn't know when I started is that what we accomplish in our chosen fields is largely dependent on how we connect to others. Connecting with heart, sharing our stories and our joy—while tapping the tools of emotional intelligence—wins the day every time. As hard data and analytics become more prevalent, personal connection, story, and meaning are even more precious and powerful, especially when we can get donors to raise their hands and say, "I want to be engaged with you in your mission."

I want to leave you with some concluding thoughts.

Never forget that *you can grow the critical skills needed to bring you from being good and competent at what you do, to being a top performer.*

It all starts with heart, as we've demonstrated throughout this book.

Once you identify your "why" and that of your staff, you can bring alive a connection to your work that may have been dormant—or just at an automatic, "dial-it-in" level—for far too long. Finding your "why" can then connect you with your personal stories, the stories of your team and your institution, and the urgent story of now.

Finding joy and messages that connect are part and parcel of emotional intelligence.

We've provided numerous guidelines and tools to put you on the path to becoming a better fundraiser, and happier person. If you are the boss or a team leader, our methods will provide you with tangible ways to grow your team while creating a cascading culture of joy, storytelling, and human capital connection. While results may not happen immediately, there is no doubt that this work will pay dividends and show up on your bottom line.

At BrightDot, we believe everything is connected. Working as one and using emotional intelligence to connect to each other is critical to having the execution necessary to be successful in our highly competitive and changing environment. Never forget that cultural change is a long-term undertaking, requiring acceptance, commitment, and grit. If you find you have the passion for this work, you must be willing to let go of the old ways and chart a new course. If you have the heart for impacting lives, and the willingness to work at it to make it better, you too can be a top-performing development officer. And so can your team.

Starting with heart—your own, the hearts of those around you, and the hearts of those people you've not yet met—can change the world. Give it a try! And let us know what happens. We'd love to hear from you.

ABOUT BILL CROUCH
AND BRIGHTDOT

Bill Crouch believes in the power of ripple effects. "For every single person's life we impact through our work, we will directly affect an exponential number of others." This principle is at the heart of BrightDot's mission and Bill's approach to life. His purpose-driven leadership style is reflective of his background in ministry, and he possesses a rare combination of creativity, authenticity, and practical knowledge to help organizations raise more money to serve more people. He approaches everything he does with a palpable energy, and finds great joy in inspiring his team and clients.

Bill honed his fundraising skills as a development director at various colleges in the Southeast, and then over 22 years as president of Georgetown College in Kentucky. He is a graduate of Wake Forest University and Southeastern Baptist Theological Seminary and is an honorary fellow at Regent's Park College at the University of Oxford. More recently, he served as the senior managing partner of Jerold Panas, Linzy & Partners. A member of the National Board of Trustees for The First Tee of the PGA Tour, Bill serves on the World Golf Foundation's Diversity Council. When he has a free afternoon, you may find him on the golf course. However, Bill is happiest when in the company of his wife, Jan, five children, and eight grandchildren.

BrightDot has assembled a diverse and talented team of experts, including another former college president; two PhDs in psychology and education; a sports psychologist; a corporate marketing director; a major university fundraiser; a published author and messaging expert; a certified executive and leadership coach; a professor of education; and a vice president of development who spearheaded a wildly successful comprehensive campaign for a leading women's college. Collectively, our core team brings more than 375 years of experience to our work.

BrightDot offers an array of fundraising consulting services, including coaching, assessments of programs and personnel (including board members), executive hiring and mentoring, strategic planning, preparation and management of fundraising campaigns, and messaging and content development to help you elevate your fundraising program. For more information about our services, contact info@thebrightdot.com.